contents

SCOTTISH WITCHES & WIZARDS

Lily Seafield

GEDDES & GROSSET

Published 2002 by Geddes & Grosset,
David Dale House, New Lanark ML11 9DJ, Scotland

© 2002 Geddes & Grosset

ISBN 1 84205 166 0

Printed and bound in the UK

introduction

The practice of magic, or witchcraft, has gone on for many centuries throughout the world. Belief in magic predates Christianity in this country by several hundred years. Its origins are in fear and uncertainty – fear of starvation, illness, death and natural disaster, uncertainty about what the future will bring, in life and after death – and the practice of magic demonstrates man's desire to bring some control into a world that is ruled by forces more powerful than himself and that he does not fully understand. Its practice continues today, having survived the onslaughts of religious and political persecution, and scientific scepticism. Over the centuries, magical practices have changed and adapted – after the spread of Christianity in Scotland, for example, we find the name of God and of the saints used in some of the incantations that were recited by witches, both 'white' and 'black'. Healer 'witches' from times long gone might be surprised if they could return today, to find that the plants used in some of their herbal remedies are widely used as a basis for modern orthodox medicines. The magic that is practised in Scotland nowadays does not necessarily have its origins in this country. We live in a multi-cultural society, and this is reflected in the diversity of ethnic origin of the occult beliefs and practices to which people subscribe. We live in the age of New Age, where belief in the occult is generally tolerated, and at worst, treated with dismissive contempt.

This was not always the case. In Europe as a whole, and Scotland in particular, there was a time when fear and hatred of magic and its practitioners reached such fever pitch that hundreds of men and women were hunted down and made to suffer terribly for alleged crimes of witchcraft. During the sixteenth and seventeenth centuries, the skies over many Scottish towns frequently clouded over with smoke from the fires that sent these people to their deaths. The exact number of those who died will never be known and many deaths will remain anonymous, but there are records surviving in sufficient quantity and quality to give us some idea of the scale of the horror. The stories of many of these people have become very well-known.

Witchcraft has provided the writers, poets and story-tellers of Scotland with a wealth of inspiration over the years. Some witch-tales are works of pure fiction, others are based on historical events, while some are legends that have built up around prominent figures in Scotland's history. They all contain elements of horror, but this is frequently laced with humour, sometimes wild imagination, and whether we believe in magic or not, most of us will admit to a fascination with stories such as these.

a charmed Life: superstition and witchcraft

Whether or not we admit to being superstitious, there are few of us who do not pay some sort of homage to superstitious practices and beliefs – we might cross our fingers or touch wood, for example, throw spilled salt over our left shoulder, or have in our possession 'lucky' items of clothing, coins, stones or talismans.

Superstitious behaviour is almost as old as man and is practised in societies in every corner of the globe. As man has struggled to forge a living in a world he does not fully understand, and against elements and occurrences over which he has little or no control, he has sought to explain the inexplicable through beliefs in external, unworldly forces; to predict the unpredictable and to control the uncontrollable through practices aimed at manipulating good and evil towards his own ends; appeasing the forces that might work against him, nurturing the forces that could benefit him.

For those who really believe in them, superstitious practices are a bit like preventative medicine. They increase the odds in your favour. It is a fact that if you do not smoke, avoid drinking to excess, eat a balanced, healthy diet and get plenty of exercise, you are less likely to die at an early age from cancer – but it is still possible. If you get a 'flu jab at the beginning of the winter, you will have some protection if an epidemic strikes – unless it is a different strain of the influenza virus. For similar reasons, a superstitious person, believing that walking under a ladder is likely to bring bad luck, will consciously avoid doing so. And just as preventative medicine cannot guarantee complete protection, and the healthy-living individual can still die prematurely from cancer, so can superstitious practice fail and the person stepping off a pavement to avoid a ladder can get knocked down by a passing bicycle. But the value of the practice of preventative medicine is rooted in science. The value of superstitious practices is rooted in the imagination. And while preventative medicine protects the individual against familiar, identifiable ills, superstitious practices are believed to protect against misfortunes that are of a much more vague and uncertain nature.

In Scottish culture there is a great wealth of customs, sayings and actions that have accumulated through centuries of superstitious belief, and many of which are still practised by people today. Some people will still plant rowan trees, believed to provide protection against evil spirits, outside their homes. When a mother takes her new baby out for the first time, neighbours and friends might still place silver coins in the prams of new infants, for giving a gift to a newborn child, especially one of silver, is thought to bring both the giver and the child good fortune. But when can a superstitious practice be considered a spell, or a charm of witchcraft?

The line between superstition and witchcraft is very faintly drawn. Perhaps one difference lies in the fact that while superstitious practices are believed to invite good fortune and ward off ill, the practice of witchcraft is thought to be capable of causing good or bad to happen. In other words, if superstition is like preventative medicine, then witchcraft is more akin to medical intervention. Witchcraft is believed to invest the practising individual with certain powers, whilst superstitious practices offer protection. Sometimes, moreover, the protection sought through superstitious practices is against the perceived evils that witches might be believed to cause. However, the two are still strongly tied to each other – they have much in common. Talismans, symbols, incantations or sayings, rituals – these are elements shared by witchcraft and superstition. It is not always clear which is which. When we see a solitary magpie and politely wish it 'good morning' to avert ill-fortune, are we merely being superstitious, or are we casting a spell?

The introduction of Christianity, and beliefs concerning mankind in relation to God (supreme good) and the Devil (supreme evil), muddies the water further. Christianity can be said to be less self-seeking than witchcraft. Christianity introduces the notion that adopting an accepted set of morals, following a certain code of behaviour, in particular in relation to God and to others, will bring benefits both in life and after death. Wonderful, or magical things, according to Christian belief, could only be achieved through God. Those who sought miracles independently of God, who performed rituals to influence their lives outwith the context of the Christian church, were performing the works of Satan. But when Christianity was introduced to Scotland, superstition was already deeply rooted, and the practice of magic already hundreds of years old. And whilst Christianity dismissed the pagan gods from the converted people's minds, it did not altogether supersede superstition. Nor did it entirely dispel beliefs in magic. Indeed, it can be argued that superstition continued to exist quite comfortably alongside Christianity in Scotland. Some of our superstitions, such as avoiding having thirteen guests seated at the same table, have their origins in the Christian religion. Many old Scottish traditional practices carried out in the celebration of milestones in life, or special festivals, combined religious belief with an abiding indulgence in superstition. For example, in some parts of

11

Scotland, where a boy and a girl were both presented for baptism on the same day, the girl had to be baptised first. If the boy's baptism were to precede the girl's, it was believed that the girl might grow a beard in later life. There were careful precautions taken for the protection of new-born infants, and certain procedures to be followed around the time of their birth, to prevent them from being taken away by fairies. When a death had taken place an equal number of precautions were taken to ensure that the spirits of the newly dead were protected from the forces of evil until a proper funeral sent them safely into the afterlife. In times gone by it was not necessarily considered enough to put your trust in God for protection against malign forces.

With the advent of Christianity, the role of the practitioners of magic gradually changed over the centuries, both in their own eyes and in the eyes of others. As far as the authorities of the Christian Church were concerned, witchcraft was heresy. Most witchcraft was now practised within the context of people's beliefs in the Christian God in Scotland, and most witches believed in God, although they might not be God-*fearing*. Traditional magical practices began to be adapted, reflecting this.

Like superstition and witchcraft, religion has its rituals, symbols, incantations and over time, we find that witches in Scotland began to integrate some elements of Christian services or prayers, albeit in perverted form, into their own practice. After the Reformation in Scotland, when the practice of Roman Catholicism was abhorred by so many leading Protestants, practitioners of magic frequently found they were considered guilty of a twofold heresy – i.e. practising witchcraft and acknowledging the rites of Roman Catholicism. Witches still commonly used, or misused, elements of the Roman Catholic mass in their rituals and charms. The idea of the Demonic pact – that witches had actively renounced their baptism and transferred their allegiances to Satan – was one which is thought to have originated in Europe and influenced Scottish witch-beliefs in the late sixteenth and early seventeenth centuries. Charges laid against accused witches and the confessions of the accused themselves, reflected how this belief had become practice. Along with the idea of the Demonic pact came that of the sabbat. Although the sabbat of the 'black' witches was not a true subversion of the Christian mass, it would frequently be conducted on sacred ground, and the prayers and incantations recited by many witches, whether these be 'white', healer witches or 'black' witches whose practice was largely malevolent and who admitted to being active devotees of Satan, frequently contained elements from, or were little more than adulterated versions of prayers that were commonly recited in the pre-Reformation Christian church.

Gradually, scepticism regarding the effectiveness and hence, the real threat of witchcraft began to overtake the fear. Whilst the church authorities might still rail against the witches as heretics and enemies God, the law makers and enforcers gradually came to the conclusion that connections like those which had been made in past years between misfortune and witchcraft were spurious, and that the practice of witchcraft itself, unless accompanied by physical violence, could not cause physical harm or death. In short, whatever the intent of the witch, whether good or evil, witchcraft did not work, and people could not commit crimes using witchcraft alone. Accordingly, the crime of witchcraft was removed from the statute books.

The period of the witch-hunts did not stamp out witchcraft in Scotland. Superstition and witchcraft alike had already shown themselves to be adaptable to change. They had modified over the centuries to absorb the influences of changing religious beliefs and practices, and of foreign witch beliefs and superstitions. In the centuries since the witch hunts, witchcraft has continued, and whilst elements of traditional magic are retained, it still continues to evolve, incorporating a fluid and changing variety of beliefs and practices into its whole.

tHe years of persecution

In 1563, during the reign of Mary, Queen of Scots, the following law was passed:

'*The Quenis Majestie and thre Estatis in this present parliament being informit that the havy, abominabill superstitioun usit be divers of the liegis of this Realme be using of Witchcraftis, Sorsarie, and Necromancie, and credence gevin thairto in tymes bygane aganis the Law of God: and for avoyding and away putting of all sic vane superstition in tymes tocum;*

it is statute and ordainit be the Quenis Majestie and thre Estatis foirsaidis that na maner of persoun nor persounis of quhatsumever estate, degre, or conditioun thay be of tak upone hand in ony tumes heirafter to use ony maner of Witchcraftis, Sorsarie, or Necromanciue: nor gif thame selfis furth to have ony sic craft or knaeledge thairof, thairthrow abusand the pepill; nor that na persoun seik ony help, response, or consultation at ony sic usaris (or abusaris) foirsaidis of Witchcraft, Sorcareis, or Necromancie, under the pane of dead: asweill to be execute aganis the user-abusar, as the seikar of the response or consultatioun.'

The practice of witchcraft, and also the consultation of those who practised witchcraft, became capital crimes. Witchcraft was a 'havy, abominabill superstitioun', 'aganis the Law of God', 'abusand the pepill'. Thus it was an offence against both God (and hence the Church) and Society.

The passing of the Act did not result in any immediate large-scale persecution, although there were a number of trials and executions between 1563 and 1590. The first 'wave' of horror began during the reign of James VI, in 1591, and lasted until 1597. It started with the trials of the witches of North Berwick, after which a General Commission was issued by the Privy Council for the trying of witches in local courts. During this period, the processing of a witch from accusation to execution was greatly simplified. Trials could go ahead without the need to apply for a commission for individual cases. Accordingly, the number of cases increased. In 1597, the General Commission was withdrawn. The king had become uneasy with the quantity of cases that were being pursued in local courts and it was suspected that personal grudges or feuds, rather than witchcraft itself, lay behind some, if not many of the prosecutions. There was a slight lull in anti-witch activities in the few years that followed, but a second wave of intense persecution took place in the late 1620's. Scotland now had a king who ruled from England. Perhaps this second wave was, in part, an indication that the State felt the need to exert its control over the people of Scotland. After another relatively quiet period there was another rise in cases of witchcraft in the 1640s. The end of the decade saw witch persecution taking off again with renewed zeal and in 1649, there was a record number of prosecutions.

During the period of Cromwell's rule in Scotland, the number of prosecutions dwindled considerably. The English judges in charge of the courts during this period showed much more scepticism towards accusations of witchcraft. Fewer cases reached prosecution and those people who were prosecuted were generally treated with greater humanity. In 1661–2, with the Protectorate over, the number of witchcraft cases brought to prosecution and the number of witch executions once more soared to a peak, but this was short-lived. The number of prosecutions leading to execution gradually declined in the final years of the seventeenth century. There were quite a few cases tried in 1697, the year in which the Paisley witches were executed, but apart from this 'blip', the trend continued downward. By the time the eighteenth century had begun, witchcraft prosecutions had become rare in most parts of Scotland. The last witch recorded as having been executed in Scotland was Janet Horne, who was burned in Dornoch in 1727. The Witchcraft Act of 1735 put an end to the terrible persecutions of the past century. The act of 1563 was repealed. Witchcraft was no longer a capital offence. In fact, the crime of witchcraft *per se* was no longer legally recognised. In its place in the new act was the crime of pretended witchcraft – the law would no longer admit of any superstition which recognised magical practices as a real or effective threat to society.

Throughout the period of the witch persecutions, the Church remained quite constant in its eagerness to hunt out and destroy its enemies. In James VI the Church found it had an ally who was equally zealous; a man who read widely on the subject and was to write his own work, *Daemonologie*, in the later years of his reign, who was given cause to see the threat of witchcraft not only as a crime against society, but as a personal offence against himself. While witches were officially regarded as enemies of the state, it is true to say that, after the reign of James VI at least, the State did not regard them with the same constancy of fear and hatred as the Church did. Furthermore, over time, there were growing indications that the legal authorities were becoming increasingly uncomfortable with the Church's abiding belief that Scotland was overrun with witches, with the manner in which suspected individuals were picked out by the accusations of neighbours, and with their subsequent treatment at the hands of the authorities in the Kirk. The Church continued to press its case against the witches, urging Parliament to do more with varying degrees of success, but the Privy Council was not always as constant as the ecclesiastical authorities in its pursuit of society's demons.

These were terrible times, and in those places in Scotland where mass trials took place and where a particularly large number of people were prosecuted, there must have been quite an atmosphere of fear, particularly amongst the female population, who were most at risk (more than nine out of ten people accused of witchcraft were women, according to surviving records). There have been many attempts to provide reasons for the severity of the witch persecution in Scotland and to explain why, although similar scenarios were being acted out in other countries in Europe at around the same time, Scotland's reaction to the perceived threat of witchcraft was particularly severe, and notably, much more severe than that of its immediate neighbour England. Some have argued that it was a manifestation of the Presbyterian Church's need to establish its authority over the people in the Post-Reformation period, and of the power struggle between Church and State. Some have linked witch-hatred with anti-Catholic sentiments prevalent at the time. Others have argued the case for misogyny, or gentry versus peasant class. Undoubtedly, the reasons that lie behind the worst periods of witch persecutions are complex. The intense wave of persecutions from 1591–97 came in the wake of a mass trial of witches who had allegedly threatened the King's life and the country's security, but treasonable witchcraft like this was almost unique and other cases brought to trial during this period and in the periods that followed mostly concerned alleged malefices of a much more personal nature. Other intense periods of witch persecution did coincide with major historical events, such as the Solemn League and Covenant (1643), and the Restoration of the Monarchy (1660), but these events in themselves are not generally considered to be the reasons why the numbers of trials in these years suddenly rose. Certain areas in Scotland suffered more than others in these periods – East Lothian, Aberdeenshire, and Fife saw a great many more witches put to their death than other areas. The north-west of Scotland remained completely free from the fear that pervaded east, central and southern Scotland. Why did the witch-panic leave such a large part of the country untouched? The reasons, geographical, social and political for the spread and severity of the Scottish witch-hunts will long be the subject of academic debate amongst historians. But there is one major factor that remained constant throughout the period, without which none of the persecutions could have taken place. The persecution of witches, wherever it took place, was possible because people at all levels of society believed in witchcraft. And as long as that belief was held to be true by both peasant and nobility, illiterate and educated, there was a focus for blame for many of the ills of society and an opportunity for figures of authority to present themselves as God's generals in the war against evil.

the Nature of a witch

I sall gang intill a hare,
Wi' sorrow, sigh and muckle care;
And I sall gang in the devil's name,
Ay while I come back again.

Changing Perceptions

From a very early age, children in our society are given the opportunity to form their own picture of what a witch is. This picture is unlikely to be drawn from any knowledge of the history of
witchcraft and people's beliefs in it. Instead, it will be drawn
from both traditional and modern fairy tales and verse, from tel-
evised drama, films and cartoons and from advertising and mar-
keting of children's toys and entertainment products. The older
stories and dramas in particular, and many of the modern ones
too, feature witches as 'baddies' – they can cast nasty spells that
change princes into frogs or make princesses fall asleep for one
hundred years. They can make life very unpleasant for their enemies. But nothing that these witches can do is irreversible. The
prince, or the fairy, or the clever child will always intervene with
perfect timing to prevent the worst from happening. Snow
White woke up; so did the Sleeping Beauty. The frog turned
back into a prince and Hansel and Gretel escaped from the gin-
gerbread house. Even the worst witches, it would seem, are not
all that bad. Moreover, for every 'evil' witch there is another who
is a figure of fun – a would-be horror who can't quite pull it off in
spite of her very best efforts – and yet another who is not bad at

all. Come Hallowe'en, the wicked witches play a starring role, with their warty faces, pointed hats and black capes, their broomsticks, cauldrons, toads and black cats. At other times of the year, the other witches are permitted, quite happily, to live alongside these old hags in the minds of our children – the good witches, always ready to reverse the malevolent magic, and the neutral witches, who look and behave just like ordinary people, but happen to be able to cast a convenient spell when the occasion demands it. The same sort of things can be said of wizards, or warlocks in children's literature and entertainment. In the most recent and highly successful addition to children's magical literature, the 'Harry Potter' series, there is a clearly defined line between good and bad magic. The central character of Harry, the boy wizard, is quite heroic, but the reader is left in doubt about the fact that some of those who possess similar powers choose to use them for the wrong reasons.

Whatever picture of a witch a child may conjure up in his or her imagination, whatever his or her idea is of what a witch can or cannot do, it is most unlikely that, in the mind of a child, even the wickedest witch will be linked in any way with any notion of the Devil, or Satanic ritual. Witches may be bad – or good – just as fairies might be; but our children, whether they believe in the existence of such people or not, will not associate them with anything they might have learnt about God and the Devil. Magic, in their minds, will have nothing to do with religion.

The modern adult perception of a witch is likely to be very different from a child's. For some adults, belief in witchcraft will be something to be dismissed as little more than a harmless eccentricity. Some will use scientific principles to argue against the possibility that magic, of any kind other than that of the illusionist, can work. Others, particularly those with strong religious faith, will have stronger objections. For them, belief in, or the practice of witchcraft is quite simply wrong.

But there are still people who call themselves witches in Scotland: 'white' witches who practise candle magic, number magic, and use spells and charms of various sorts. There are also many who do not consider themselves to be witches, but who subscribe to practices that could be said to fall under the umbrella term of witchcraft: fortune-telling, tarot, healing or spiritualism for example. There are also others who practise the Black Arts; who consciously reject the teachings of the Christian church and embrace Satanism. In modern society, these people might be frowned upon, some of them might give us cause to fear that our children will be influenced by their ideas, but they cannot be prosecuted for their beliefs. They are permitted to carry out their rituals without fear of punishment unless any of their actions constitutes a criminal offence.

In sixteenth- and seventeenth-century Scotland any distinction between 'white' and 'black' magic became irrelevant, and any notion of magic working independently of either God or the Devil was dismissed. The practice of magic was the work of the Devil, God's greatest foe. Curing, harming, charming, cursing, foretelling the future and talking to spirits of the dead were equally suspect activities. Those who claimed to do any such things, those who were seen to do any such things, and those who were said to have done any such things were equally liable to find themselves in danger from the wrath of the church authorities and the courts.

The Hunted

What was a witch, in the eyes of those who led the witch hunts of the sixteenth and seventeenth centuries? Who were these people who were persecuted in their hundreds? Is there a handful of criteria that we can look for, in order to identify the sort of person who typically fell foul of the church and the courts – the likely suspects? How many of them were guilty of practising witchcraft? If they were all guilty as charged, then we would have to assume that witchcraft had reached epidemic proportions in Scotland; but were Church and State responding to a real epidemic of evil in their midst, or was witchcraft no more commonly practised than it had ever been?

The statistics that can be calculated from surviving records of witch trials reveal, to a certain extent, certain factors that were held in common by a significant number of the accused.

Firstly, although men were prosecuted for witchcraft, it is true to say that the majority of those who were tried for such crimes were women. Throughout the period of witch persecutions, around eighty per cent of those suspected of witchcraft were female. This is sometimes interpreted as sign of women's inferior status in society, or of 'institutional misogyny' on the part of the church and the courts. But the figures may simply illustrate social perceptions of witchcraft at the time; it was seen primarily as a woman's crime. That is to say, because of the things that people believed to be true about witches, women were more likely suspects, and therefore more women were apprehended.

Members of the wealthy or noble classes, although less vulnerable when it came to a trial because of the position and influence they held in society, were not entirely untouched by the pointing fingers of the witch-hunters. Nonetheless, statistics show that members of the upper classes were less likely to be accused in the first place. Most of the accused came from the poorer classes. Many were widows – and thus likely to be financially compromised. Others were frequently the wives of craftsmen, low wage-earners, or poor tenant farmers. Some had been reduced to the status of a beggar. But in spite of the fact that most accused witches in Scotland were obviously far from wealthy, and might have had little status, they were nonetheless likely to have fixed residence, at least, in the community from which the accusations against them stemmed. Some vagabonds and itinerant workers were prosecuted for witchcraft, but the majority of suspects were settled in one place. The importance of reputation in Scottish witchcraft trials, discussed later in this book, helps to account for this. Reputations built up over a period of time; the itinerant workers or vagabonds only stayed for short periods at a time in any one place, and thus, there was less time for suspicious reputations to take root and become established.

The age of a 'typical' Scottish witch is not so easy to tell. Some were old, some were little more than girls, but there are indications that the majority of those who were accused were in the 'middle-age' bracket. Most were married, or widowed, and were therefore clearly adults. Several had children, many of whom were adults themselves. There were certainly several old women who found themselves on trial for witchcraft during the period, but any notion of the typical Scottish witch of the sixteenth and seventeenth centuries being a wizened old hag would be wrong.

How many of those persecuted were guilty of knowingly practising what they believed to be witchcraft? This question is impossible to answer with any great degree of certainty for a number of reasons.

Firstly, the confessions of accused witches cannot be taken at face value. During the sixteenth and seventeenth centuries, a confession from the accused was often taken as adequate proof of guilt, no matter how bizarre the nature of the confession. But without knowing the nature of the questions asked of the accused, or the manner in which they were asked (and with how much force), without knowing something of the mental state of the accused, both before and after confession, we cannot accept the content of any of these confessions as fact. Most confessions were quite likely to have been extracted under conditions that would nowadays be considered prejudicial. Several condemned witches publicly recanted their confessions as they were about to be put to death. What had they to gain by doing this if they were guilty? It is true that there were plenty of men and women who admitted to the foulest and weirdest of deeds, but (putting aside the physical impossibility of some of the things that they claimed to have done) there are still more reasons for not accepting their admissions than there are for taking them as truth.

Isobel Gowdie famously testified in 1662 that she could turn herself into a hare. Why? There are a number of possible reasons. She may have been deranged, either before, or as a result of her interrogation, and have believed what she said to be true. Perhaps she knew it was not true, but felt that something like this was what they (her interrogators) wanted to hear – the idea might have been suggested to her, or even forced upon her. Perhaps, in some bizarre way, she wanted the notoriety which she must have known she would earn from having made such a statement. It may have been something said as a last mocking gesture of defiance in the face of her inevitable doom. Did she practise the black arts? She may well have done. But her confession reveals to us little about what she was really like; instead, it tells us more about what people were willing to believe to be true of her. People believed in the power of witchcraft – and some people believed they could achieve things through practising witchcraft. But this does not mean that all those who eventually confessed to practising witchcraft were guilty of it.

The charges laid against accused witches pose their own difficulties. Firstly, they were likely to be as incredible as the confessions. (One might argue that through force, or leading questions, the interrogators of many suspects quite possibly made every effort to ensure that confessions fitted accusations). The last witch to be legally executed in Scotland, Janet Horne, who was burned at Dornoch in 1722, was accused of having had her daughter shod by the Devil and having ridden her through the air like a horse to meet the Black Master himself. Why would such a story be told in court and received with any credulity? And yet the charges laid against Janet Horne were no more bizarre than many other accusations made against similar people in her position. We may find it astonishing that such stories were ever taken seriously, but it must be remembered that belief in the real, effective power of witchcraft was prevalent in Scotland at that time. There were differences in the content and detail of belief. That is to say, there was not one fixed view about exactly how a witch might operate, what powers he or she might have and how they might be used. Nor was the notion of a witch as one who had made a pact with the Devil always universally held. But it must be recognised that, although there must have been some people who were sceptical about the real threat of witchcraft, belief in witches was widespread throughout all ranks of society. This belief was the essential precondition for the persecution of the witches. If people could do harm or ill by magic, or by harnessing the power of Satan, then it was possible for them to have done more than this. . .to have flown, to have changed form, to have communicated with the dead, etc.

The charges laid against many suspect witches were often the result of certain facts being linked with current beliefs about witchcraft. In the case of Janet Horne, for example, her daughter had deformed feet. It is likely also, that for some reason Janet Horne's lifestyle or character had aroused suspicion within the community. Witches were believed to have the power to change people, or objects, into magical vehicles to transport them to their meetings. And so the connection would be made between Janet Horne, witchcraft, and her daughter. Many other trials for witchcraft involved similar connections between fact and belief. Frequently the connection was made between illness, or death, and witchcraft. Witches were believed capable of causing both, and therefore when a sudden illness could not be explained, and a suspect person had been near, or had said something, the illness would be attributed to witchcraft and the finger of blame would point at the suspect person. Now it may be that in some cases, the person who was accused of causing the illness had actually intended harm to the victim. But the fact that the accusers made a connection between what they believed possible and their feelings of unease (for whatever reason) about a certain individual does not mean that the individual – even if subsequently found guilty – was guilty of practising witchcraft.

Some accused witches may have found themselves on trial for reasons other than genuine suspicions within their community.

Some accusations of witchcraft may have been actions of malice, and the evidence presented against the accused sheer fiction. What better way to exact revenge upon someone you despise? Such accusations might have been motivated by mistrust, personal feuds, politics – any one of a number of reasons why one or more people might wish harm to one or more others, or, quite simply, want them disposed of permanently. In the famous case of the North Berwick witch trials, which are dealt with in another chapter of this book, one of the accused (who was fortunate to escape with his life) was Francis Stewart, Earl of Bothwell. While there have been suggestions that he did have a certain interest in matters of an occult nature, it is, however, almost certain that his arrest was politically motivated. Witch or no witch, he posed a threat to the king. He was implicated in the case by others who had already been made to confess their own part in the affair – and the king had taken a personal interest in their interrogation. Who mentioned Bothwell's name first – accusers or accused?

It is even possible that some accusations may have arisen, not because of genuine or well-founded suspicion of a certain individual, but because of the accusers' own fear of persecution. During the period of the witch-hunts, and especially at their height, there was undoubtedly a climate of fear in those parts of Scotland that were most affected. Once one witch had been accused, it was not uncommon for those close to her to find themselves facing similar charges. Husbands, children, neighbours or friends could find themselves in a very vulnerable position. Who would be accused next? It is only a matter of conjecture, but it is not unreasonable to accept the possibility that, urged from the pulpit by over-zealous ministers to seek out the evil ones in their community, some people might make the decision that it was safer to join the ranks of the accusers than to put themselves at risk of becoming one of the accused. Charges of witchcraft frequently arose as a result of accusations being made against other people by confessants. It was generally assumed that witches did not act alone; they would have others in their covey, or coven. Having admitted to her (or his) own guilt, it was common practice for a so-called witch to be persuaded, or forced, to implicate several others. These accusations were generally treated with some caution, for a confessed witch was not thought to be a reliable witness. The investigating authorities would look for further corroborating evidence before prosecution. But even when investigations led to a successful prosecution, a guilty verdict cannot be accepted by us as proof of guilt, for the same reasons as those outlined above. The accusations, like the confessions of those who had made them, were likely to have been made under extremes of duress, and were unreliable. Further evidence collected against the accused, as we have already seen, would frequently consist of dubious connections being made between belief and circumstance, or might be made out of malice or fear.

In some cases, of course, in addition to the confessions of the guilty party and the verbal evidence of others, there would be physical evidence that the accused was indeed a practising witch. Such evidence might consist of wax or clay images, commonly used in magic, or talismans, charms and suchlike. This can be accepted as 'hard' evidence that the accused, was guilty of practising witchcraft. And in some cases, even with the absence of such hard evidence, it seems, on balance of probability, most likely that the accused did see her (or himself) as a witch, and did practise magic, for good or for evil.

There were many practising witches in Scotland at the time of the persecutions, and some of them were among those who faced the penalty for their crimes. But of the total number of those who were tried, we cannot tell how many were truly guilty as charged.

So we know that most witch suspects were poor, most were middle-aged and most were female. Some were practising witches, attempting to heal or to harm, to do good or evil through magical practices. Is there anything else that can contribute to this hazy picture of a 'typical' witch of sixteenth and seventeenth century Scotland?

There are definite indications that suggest that a certain type of character was more likely to face accusations of malefice than others. Time after time, records of trials show that many accusations resulted directly from disputes. Typically, following a dispute between the accused and some other, one of the following would happen:

1) The accused would utter a curse, or at least words that were taken as a curse.
2) The accused would utter a curse, and some time afterwards

something bad would happen to the other party in the dispute, which was then understood as being the curse taking effect.

3) Something bad would happen to the other party in the dispute, and although cursing had not been heard, it was assumed that it had been done, or that the accused had cast the evil eye on the other party.

A single scenario such as this, presented as evidence, would not necessarily be considered sufficient to indicate the guilt of the accused, but it was generally the case that there would be two or more similar accounts, given by different witnesses against the accused. Some suspects, notably Agnes Finnie of Edinburgh, found themselves facing a long list of charges arising from past disputes, curses, and subsequent calamities. Records of trials show that people's memories were not short, for some of these charges would relate to incidents that had taken place several years previously.

Given this knowledge about the trials, it is safe to assume that many of the women who became suspects were argumentative souls. Whether they had a justifiable complaint to make or were just fiery-tempered and quick to take offence, they were not the sort of person to take a perceived slight lying down. Clearly, sometimes their tongues ran away with them. Whether their curses were spoken with real intent or not, they were likely to regret them in time.

Sometimes, of course, the real malevolence of an accused witch was not in question. Such was the case of Lady Foulis. Her malefice did not manifest itself in the hastily spoken curse. When a family dispute moved her to resort to witchcraft, she turned to poisons and image magic. Lady Foulis was a wealthy and influential woman and as such, did not conform to the picture of a 'typical' witch. But as far as her temper goes, we can safely assume that she had at least this much in common with many others who were tried.

Was the 'typical' witch a solitary creature, a friendless, misunderstood eccentric who spoke to no-one and kept themselves to themselves? In many cases, the contrary was true. Although some might have been reclusive figures, or widows left alone in the world, the records show that many witch suspects were obviously very much a part of the community in which they lived, who knew and were known by the people in the neighbourhood well enough to be on speaking terms at least, and often well enough to ask for or to offer assistance in times of need. Sometimes they had been healers, accepted within the community so long as their healing powers were seen to be effective and so long as healing did not turn to harm. Sadly, all too often accusations of witchcraft arose from the suspect's interaction with others going awry.

There is another factor that indicates the unlikelihood of the 'typical' witch being a loner. In many ways witchcraft was believed to be, and was, according to the confessions of many witches, quite a social activity. Many of the alleged malefices of accused witches were not practised alone, but in the company of one or more people. The confessions of Agnes Sampson of North Berwick and Isobel Gowdie of Auldearn are just two of several to indicate that witches were quite likely to perform their magic in groups, and that witches' meetings could quite boisterous activities, attended not necessarily by a small select few, but by several. They were occasions not just for dark and devilish deeds, but also for fun. Some witches may have been lonely women, attracted to witchcraft by the prospect of company and excitement, but they were not necessarily solitary people by nature.

Some suspects might, nowadays, be labelled 'eccentric', or 'mad'. Some may even have been suffering from paranoia or delusions. But there is nothing in the information to be gathered from existing records to allow us to estimate with any accuracy what proportion of those taken to trial fell into either the eccentric or psychotic categories.

The picture that can be drawn of a 'typical' witch can only be very roughly sketched. While you were more likely to be accused of witchcraft if you were a poor, middle-aged woman with a quick temper and a foul mouth – and even more at risk if you were a healer, or did practise witchcraft – it must be acknowledged that hundreds of those who were brought to trial did not fit these criteria.

If there is one thing that can be said to be true of all the alleged witches who were prosecuted in Scotland in the sixteenth and seventeenth centuries, whether they saw themselves as witches or not, it is perhaps that they were all people who (through their own fault or otherwise) found themselves with enemies, and who then fell foul of a belief that pervaded all ranks of society at the time: the belief that witchcraft entailed real and *effective* practices, that could be used for good or for evil. Had that belief not been as prevalent as it was, whether they were innocent of practising witchcraft or guilty, these people could never have been successfully prosecuted in such large numbers. Had that belief not been as prevalent as it was, we might argue that it is unlikely that the Witchcraft Act of 1563 would ever have been passed.

the magic of witches

Disease and its cure, death and a huge variety of misfortunes have been attributed to the power of witchcraft in Scotland's past. A long list of very specific rites, spells and practices accumulated over the years, which were associated with the magic of a witch or a wizard.

There are a number of things that are particularly important in the lives of human beings. Some are universally so. The desire to live as long as possible is driven by a primitive survival instinct, present in all humans. Freedom from sickness and injury and an adequate supply of food and drink are universally desired as they will increase longevity. The desire for sex, which stems from an animal instinct to procreate, but which Man of all creatures finds singularly pleasurable, is virtually universal. Romantic love, happiness and wealth are important to and sought after by a significantly large proportion of human beings. The magic of witches revolved round all these things, affecting them either to people's benefit or to their loss. In addition to this, witches had one more card to play: they could tempt people away from God, into the arms of Satan and towards certain eternal damnation.

Health, Sickness and Death

'I forbid the quaking fevers, the sea fevers, the land fevers and all the fevers that ever God ordained, out of the head, out of the heart, out of the back, out of the sides, out of the knees, out of the thighs, from the

points of the fingers to the tips of the toes: out shall the fevers go, some to the hill, some to the hap, some to the stone, some to the stock. In Saint Peter's name, Saint Paul's name, and all the saints of Heaven, in the name of the Father, the Son, and the Holy Ghost.'

Many witches made a reputation for themselves in the first place because of their perceived abilities to cure the sick. In retrospect, we can recognise that in some cases, the recovery of the sick person and the charms of the witch would be no more than coincidental. Whatever the witch may have done, the sickness was of such a kind that the person was likely to recover anyway. In other cases, a person's healing abilities will have come from a knowledge of the properties of those herbs which are now known to have proven medicinal effects. But in times gone by, the herbs were seen as an adjunct to the witches' powers, rather than the source of relief in themselves. Thus, when a witch was consulted about a sick cow or an ailing child, it was the person who mixed the medicaments and the charms that he or she uttered that brought about the cure. If herbs were used, they were only part of the magic. Other rituals, such as washing the garments of the sick person in south-running water (for only south-running water had magical powers) might be carried out and rhymes and invocations could also be used as part of the process of healing.

Witches were believed to be able not only to cure illnesses completely, but to remove sickness from one person and transfer it to another. Nowadays we can see that in all probability, the transference of illness from one person to another (where it really happened) was more likely to have been the result of infection or contagion than anything a third party might have brought about by magic.

When a witch was crossed, the magic of curing could turn to

the magic of causing disease, or even of killing. The revenge was not always taken out directly on the person who had caused offence, but on someone close to them, or on one of their livestock. Frequently, when a member of a family fell sick or died, this event was seen as the result of that person, or others in the family, having angered a reputed witch. Child deaths were not uncommon. It is a fact that children are more vulnerable to disease than adults, and in the sixteenth and seventeenth centuries children were much more likely to die in the first ten years of life than they are nowadays. Living conditions, particularly in the towns, were insanitary. Medical knowledge was scant and the importance of hygiene in preventing the spread of disease was not recognised. There were epidemics of diseases such as smallpox and measles, from which our own children are protected by immunisation in modern times. The sixteenth and seventeenth centuries also saw both plague and famine strike Scotland. The same lack of medical expertise that failed to preserve the lives of so many children also allowed superstitious fears to flourish. Consequently, when a child became ill or died – whether it be with gastro-enteritis, smallpox, scarlet fever or something else – and a bad-tempered neighbour had quarrelled with the child's parents in recent memory, the parents were quite likely to suspect the neighbour of having caused the child's illness. Equally, if a farmer fell out with a reputed witch and his cows suddenly fell sick, or stopped producing milk, the witch would fall under suspicion immediately.

In 1661, a husband and wife from Elgin, John Rind and Elspeth Smith, were brought before the Kirk Session accused of charming. Several people testified against them and the charges involved both curing and causing sickness. Elspeth was said to have bought a stone from another man; a white stone which was believed to have magical properties. Although

Elspeth denied using the stone herself, she admitted that it had magical properties and knew it to have been used by other men, whom she named, to cure a sick cow. Elspeth was also said to have used charms on a sick baby, telling them that the baby would either live or die soon. Her husband John faced similar charges, all of which he denied. Specifically, a man called Robert Hardie testified that John had asked a favour of him, and he had refused. Following his refusal to oblige John, his baby had become ill:

'At the said John Rind's coming to the house, howsoone he went to the doore, the chyld took greit seiknes and did swell and wrought nyne dayes daylie and hourlie lyk to die. . .'

So far, the charges are quite typical of many accusations made against witch suspects. The second part of Robert Hardie's testimony demonstrates the belief that if illness has been caused by a witch, the same witch can also remove the illness:

'. . .and the said Robert being in suspitione of the said John went to him and sent for him and howsoone he looked one the child he thereafter within ane schort space came to perfect health.'

It seems that certain kinds of ailment were particularly prone to give rise to suspicions of witchcraft. These include fits, fevers, swelling of the body, paralysis and loss of speech in humans, and bloody milk (probably mastitis) or loss of milk in cattle.

There were numerous rituals, rhymes and invocations that could be used for the laying on, taking off or transference of sickness. Sickness or death could be achieved with merely a look, if someone had the Evil Eye. The Auldearn witches, according to Isobel

Gowdie had quite a collection of doggerel at their disposal, whether they wanted to cure or to kill. Both they and the North Berwick witches made up bags of toad venom, nail clippings and other strange ingredients to use against their victims. They also made use of image magic.

Image Magic

Attempting to harm or even kill an individual using a wax or clay image, or even a picture of that person, is a practice that is not unique to Scottish witchcraft. Similar practices can be found in old magic rituals in several countries worldwide. Several Scottish witches were charged with having used this kind of malefice during the period of the great witch hunts. The image might be roasted over a fire or even burned, or have pins stuck in it to cause fever, pain or disease in the corresponding areas of the intended victim's body. Sometimes the finished figure would be placed in a stream, and as the clay gradually dissolved, it was believed that the intended victim would waste away.

The North Berwick witches used both figurines and pictures to try to kill King James VI in 1589–90. Isobel Gowdie of Auldearn and others in her coven constructed one clay figure with which they intended to kill all the sons of the Laird of Park. Her description of what they did with the figure was quite precise:

We laid the face of it to the fire till it strakened and a clear fire round about it till it was red like a coal. After that we would roast it now and then. Each other day there would be a piece of it weel rosten. The Laird of Park's whole male children by it are to suffer, if it be not gotten and broken, as well as those that are born and dead already. It was still put in and taken out of the fire in the Devil's name. It was hung upon an knag. It is yet in John Taylor's house, and it has a cradle of clay about it.'

Lady Katherine Foulis, tried, but acquitted, for witchcraft in Edinburgh in 1537, was another who allegedly used image magic for harm. She was accused of having made several figures of her stepson Robert as part of her plan to kill him.

The Taking of Milk, Stealing and Spoiling of Crops, Fish and Other Food

> *Thence, countra wives, wi' toil an' pain,*
> *May plunge an' plunge the kirn in vain;*
> *For Oh! the yellow treasure's ta'en*
> *By witching skill;*
> *An' dawit, twal-pint Hawkie's gane*
> *As yell's the Bill.*

Robert Burns, *Address to the Deil*

Food is universally important for the maintenance of life and in times when many people found themselves frequently going hungry, any threat to their supply of food, or their means of earning an income from which they might buy food, was greatly feared. It is not surprising, therefore, that many beliefs about the magic of witches concerned the taking of food, or the interrupting of its supply. Witches terrorised the farmer or smallholder. They spoiled the crops, they stole the produce, they stopped the hens from laying. Anything that the farmer might achieve in byre or field through the sweat of his brow, could be undone in the wink of an eye by the magic of a witch.

Witches were frequently accused of taking milk from their neighbours' cows. This theft could be achieved, apparently, without the witch having to step over her own threshold. A 'harry tedder' (hairy tether) was quite commonly used. This was a sort of plaited rope, made from the tail hair of one, or several cows. Having made such a device, the witch only had to wave it over her own milk churn or twist it, in order to obtain a good supply of milk from her neighbour. Alternatively, the witch might wave the tether between the legs of the cow to produce milk.

A wooden pin or peg might also be used. This would be stuck into a place in the wall of the witch's house and turned. A stream of milk would then flow from the pin into a suitably placed receptacle. Janet Wishart of Aberdeen was charged, among other things, with the taking of milk. Elspeth McKewn of Dalry was said to have a magical wooden pin that she kept in the wall of her cottage. If she took the pin to her neighbour's cow and placed it against an udder, she could get all the milk she wanted.

There is an old story told in the Borders about the magical theft of milk, very much the traditional tale of the Magic Porridge Pot. Some workmen visiting a farm in the Borders were intrigued by the generous supply of milk that was available to them when they sat down to eat. Whenever the milk pitcher was emptied, the farmer's wife would pick it up and leave the room for a few moments, returning with it filled to the brim once more. The next time the pitcher was emptied, one wily lad followed her and saw her go up to a peg that had been hammered into the gable end wall of the house, and twist it. Milk poured from the peg into the pitcher and when the pitcher was full, the farmer's wife simply twisted the peg again and the milk stopped.

Later on in the day, the workers were hot, tired and thirsty, but the farmer's wife was nowhere to be seen to ask for a drink. The lad who knew her secret decided to impress his fellow workers, and took the milk pitcher over to the peg in the wall. He twisted the peg and, sure enough, milk started pouring out. The pitcher was filled in no time and the lad gave the peg a twist ... but the milk would not stop. He called his workmates to help him and in spite of all their efforts, they could not get the milk to stop flowing from the peg. They gathered all the cups, bowls and pans they could find in the house and before long, every available container was full to the brim. The farmer's wife came home just in time to stop her house from being flooded with milk, and ranted and raved at the workmen for depriving all the farmers in the district of a day's produce from their cows. It was the last time the workmen were offered a drink of milk in that farm.

Witches were also believed to be able to affect a cow's ability to produce milk and to be able to spoil the milk that was produced and the dittays against several accused witches reflect these beliefs. Isobel Young from East Lothian, who was charged with witchcraft in 1629, was said to have bewitched a cow so that for three days, it gave red blood instead of milk. Another witch, Marioun Peebles, was said to have stopped her neighbour's cows from producing milk for thirteen days altogether.

Human milk could be affected by witchcraft in a similar way. Bessie Roy from Aberdeenshire was charged in 1590 with, amongst other things, the

'*abstracking. . . of wemmennis milk (and) bestis milk*'.

Bessie had caused the milk of a nurse called Bessie Steill to dry up.

When the milk was of poor quality, and butter would not churn properly, witchcraft was commonly believed to be the cause (see the extract from *Address to the Deil*, above).

Farming will always be a risky occupation. The success or failure of a year's crop depends on several different factors in addition to the skill of the farmer; the quality of the seed and the land, the (notoriously unreliable) weather, the presence or absence of crop diseases and pests. Modern farmers have scientific research on their side; meteorologists predict weather changes helping the farmers to plan the best times for crop sowing and harvesting. Growers are now equipped with scientific knowledge of the principles of crop rotation and of the soil nutrients and weather conditions, etc., that are necessary for successful cultivation of certain crops. They also know the practical methods by which soil can be improved, and for those who choose to use them, there are chemicals available in abundance to kill crop pests and diseases and fertilise the soil.

In Scotland in the sixteenth and seventeenth centuries, farming, whether on a relatively large scale or on one or two acres, was much more difficult. Crop failures, for whatever reason, posed a real threat to the prosperity of a community and a poor year could cause a smallholder considerable hardship. It is understandable therefore, that at that time, when agricultural science was barely in its infancy, witchcraft was blamed for many a diseased crop or poor harvest. The belief that witches could damage crops with their magic was compounded by some self-acknowledged witches, who admitted in their confessions to having attempted to cause such havoc, and seemed to believe that they had succeeded. Isobel Gowdie of Auldearn told how she and her fellow-witches took action against a farmer by the name of Broadley:

'John Taylor and Janet Breadhead, his wife, . . . and I myself, met in the kirkyard of Nairn, and we raised an unchristened child out of its

grave; and at the end of Broadley's corn field land. . . . we took the said child, with the nails of our fingers and toes, pickels of all sorts of grain, and blaids of kail, and hacked them all very small, together. And did put a part thereof among the muck-heaps of Broadley's lands, and thereby took away the fruit of his corns, and we parted it among our two covins.'

So it was that the food was taken from the plates of those who had worked to produce it.

The Sinking of Ships

In coastal areas, where fishing provided both nourishment and income for the inhabitants, the loss of ships and fishermen affected communities dreadfully. Many of the witch trials in sixteenth and seventeenth century Scotland took place in coastal towns and frequently, the charges involved the sinking, or the attempted sinking of ships. The North Berwick witches famously planned for King James VI's ship to be sunk on its homeward voyage from Denmark. They did not succeed in this, but they did sink one of the accompanying craft, along with its cargo of wedding gifts. It was alleged in the trial of Elizabeth Bathgate of Eyemouth that she and her witch cronies had sunk the ship belonging to George Hynd, killing him and his crew and losing the cargo. Elizabeth Bathgate, like the North Berwick witches, had caused her deadly havoc with the help of Satan. Amongst the evidence gathered for the trial of those accused of tormenting Christian Shaw of Bargarran, there was a tale of the sinking of a ferry, drowning captain and crewman. Similar stories were told in trials from Shetland in the north to Berwick in the south. It was widely believed that it was possible to raise a storm or a heavy mist with the use of magic, and even when there were no suspects on whom to lay the blame, fierce or freak weather conditions, especially those resulting in the loss of boats and lives, were frequently attributed to sorcery. Sometimes a ship might sink for no apparent reason; no wind sufficiently strong to dash the vessel upon the rocks or cause it to overturn, no fog to make navigation difficult. What else might have caused the disaster? Witchcraft had to be the answer.

In cases where fishing boats survived to return to their home ports, even in spite of stormy weather, but returned from their voyages with few fish to show for their labours, witchcraft was again sometimes thought to be the reason. Witches, it was believed, could take the fish from the nets of fishing boats by magic, filling their own stomachs with the stolen haul.

Weather Predicting and Weather Changing

The belief in the possibility of changing the weather by magic did not only affect those who lived on the coast. In rural areas, where so many families were dependent upon the land for their living, favourable weather conditions were all important. Ruined harvests were often blamed on witchcraft. Weather predicting was also regarded as a suspicious activity – a sign of witchcraft rather than any talent for reading the signs in nature. And for every person who claimed he or she could predict the weather or affect the elements, there were several more who were prepared to believe them. Isobel Gowdie told, in her confession, how she and her fellow-witches could raise the wind:

'When we raise the wind, we takes a rag of cloth and wets it in water, and we takes a beetle (a wooden bat for beating the laundry) *and knocks the rag on a stone, and we say thrice over:*

' "*I knock this rag upon this stane,*
To raise the wind in the devil's name,
It shall not lie until I please again."

'*When we would lay the wind, we dry the rag, and say thrice over:*

' "*We lay the wind in the Devil's name,*
Not to rise till we like to raise it again." '

Janet Wishart of Aberdeen was another witch who was said to be able to raise or lay the wind. The relevant part of her indictment reads as follows:

'*Thou art indicted and accused for practising of thy witchcraft in laying of the wind and making of it to become calm and louden, a special point teached to thee by thy master Satan, whilk thou did in this form: taking of ane beatle in the craig toun of Lunfanan, and hanging up of the beatle by ane string or thread, and whispering thereon thy devilish orisons by a certain space, through the whilk thy devilish witchcraft so used by thee, the wind – that blew loud, the whilk no man for the greatness and vehemency thereof could hold his feet upon the ground – became calm and low.*'

Shape-Shifting

It was commonly believed that witches could change, if so desired, into the shapes of various other creatures. Sometimes this was done in order to transport themselves from one place to another. At other times, it was done to achieve their evil ends more effectively – to enable them to enter people's houses without being recognised, for example. It is relatively easy to rationalise such beliefs if they were only held by the accusers. One explanation might go as follows. Misfortune strikes a certain household.

A child falls suddenly, inexplicably and seriously ill. A local woman, a witch by reputation, is suspected of having caused the child harm. She has not been seen around the home of the child, but an unfamiliar black cat was noticed close to where the child lay sleeping just before illness struck. The cat becomes the witch in the eyes of the child's family – a Satanic servant metamorphosed for the purposes of avoiding detection while carrying out her master's deeds.

But how did it come about that several confessed witches described how they were changed into other creatures – ravens, hares, cats – and appeared to believe that this was the case? It has been suggested that if confessants did literally volunteer the information, believing it to be true, and had not been forced to come up with such stories, then hallucinogenic substances might have been used at witches' meetings which gave those who consumed them the conviction that they had been transformed. This theory might hold some truth, but it does not explain the relative uniformity of the stories. Three creatures, the cat, the raven or crow and the hare, the most common of which was the cat, featured consistently. Whatever possible explanations there might be for this phenomenon, we have to accept that it was the case that often both accusers and the accused believed that shape-changing could, and did, take place. Isobel Gowdie of Auldearn claimed she could change into a hare by reciting a rhyme. By the same means she could also change into a raven or a cat whenever the need arose, she said. Isobel Young was accused by her husband of turning into a cat and coming out of a hole in the roof of the house. Marie Lamont of Inverkip confessed that she and others had changed into cats more than once.

If a witch was wounded whilst in the shape of another creature, the wound would remain when she changed herself back into human form. Isobel Gowdie told her accusers how, when she and her fellow witches were in the shape of hares:

> '*The dogs will sometimes get bites of us, when we are in hares but will not get us killed; when we turn out of a hare's likeness in our own shape, we will have the bites, and rives, and scratts in our bodies.*'

Love

Witches, it was believed, could affect your love life for better and for worse. They had ways of making one person fall romantically for another, the magical means to make one person seem more attractive to another and charms and potions to aid fertility. But they could also destroy what love there might have been between two people. They could cause a woman to lose her ability to bear children, or make a man impotent. *Newes from Scotland,* the pamphlet published shortly after the prosecution of the North Berwick Witches, contains an account of one witch's love spell that went wrong after interference from another party. The account was part of the evidence collected to convict John Fian, the schoolmaster from Prestonpans, of witchcraft, and stands out from the horrors of the rest of the trial as a bizarrely comic incident. John Fian was attracted to the sister of one of his school pupils and set about gaining her love by magical means. He needed some of the girl's hair to carry out his magic, and asked the girl's brother to get some for him. The boy agreed to do as he was asked, and tried to take some hairs from his sister as she was sleeping, but every time he tried, he woke her up. The girl, understandably irritated by her brother's behaviour, complained to her mother. Having some knowledge of witchcraft herself, the mother suspected what might be going on and questioned her son about the matter. When she discovered that the boy was acting on behalf of John Fian, she took some hairs from a cow and gave these to her son to take to him. Fian, believing the hairs belonged to the boy's sister, carried out his love magic on them. Shortly afterwards he found himself being pursued by an amorous cow everywhere he went, much to the amusement of onlookers.

Elf-Shot

'I charge thee for arrowschot,
For doorschot, for wombschot,
For liverschot, for lungschot,
For hertschote, all the maist;
In the name of the Father, the Sone, and Haly Ghaist.
To wend out of flesch and bane,
In to stick and stane,
In the name of the Father, the Sone and Haly Ghaist, Amen.'

Cure for elf-shot cattle, recited by Bartie Paterson at her trial in 1607.

Elf-shot were small flint arrows, now thought in reality to be Neolithic arrows that were commonly found around old burial-sites dating from that period. It was at one time believed that these were used as magical weapons, fired at their victims by elves, and also by witches. Isobel Gowdie of Auldearn clearly believed in their efficacy, and claimed not only to have used them, but to have had first-hand knowledge of their manufacture; the arrows, she said were sharpened by the Devil's own hand and were then passed on to the elves for finishing. She had seen this being done for herself when she was in Elfland.

Elf-arrows, she said, were fired by the elves with bows, but witches fired them by flicking them with their thumbnails. No-one saw them being fired, but it was believed that elf arrows flew about in the air after dark, and could cause all sorts of havoc among beasts and humans. It was believed that elf-arrows did not leave a hole in the skin of the victim. The only sign that they had pierced a body might be a small blue mark, which was hard to detect. Nevertheless, the harm that they could do was not to be underestimated. They could cause great sickness, sometimes even death, or so it was said. Inexplicable disease in people and animals – cattle in particular – was frequently attributed to elf-shot, and the Devil and his servants were blamed.

Witches and the Devil

> *Let warlocks grim, an wither'd Hags,*
> *Tell, how wi you, on ragweed nags,*
> *They skim the muirs an dizzy crags,*
> *Wi wicked speed;*
> *And in kirkyards renew their leagues,*
> *Owre howkit dead.*

Robert Burns, *Address to the Deil*

> *There sat Auld Nick, in shape o'beast;*
> *A touzie tyke, black, grim and large*

Robert Burns *Tam o' Shanter*

As far as the Church and State in Post-Reformation Scotland were concerned, witchcraft was the greatest enemy that they faced. Witches were the servants of the Devil. From the 1590s onwards, the Kirk Sessions and courts sought to prove the link between accused witches and the Devil by searching for evidence, or extracting a confession from the accused, that a Demonic Pact had been made; that the accused had formally put herself or himself in the service of Satan. The first stage of the pact was the renouncal of baptism. The confessions of some witches told how this was done. With one hand on the opposite foot and the other hand on the head, the convert would state their renouncal, usually at a Sabbat, a witches' meeting, at which the Devil was present. The pact was sealed with the Devil making his mark somewhere about the witch's person, either with his hand (nipping) or mouth (kissing, licking or biting). The mark was generally made in a place where it would be hidden from general sight – under clothing, under hair, or even in the mouth.

The Rev. Robert Kirk described his knowledge of witch-marks as follows:

"A spot that I have seen, as a small mole, horny and brown coloured; throw which mark, when a large pin was thrust (both in buttock, nose and rooff of mouth), till it bowed and became crooked, the witches, both men and women, nather felt a pain or did bleed, nor know the precise time when this was doing to them (their eyes only be covered)."

Some witches said that the marking was painful and that the pain lasted for some time, until the Devil passed his hand over the spot again, relieving the discomfort.

Amongst the confessions given by accused witches and the accusations made against them, were some stories of sexual intercourse taking place between female witches and their new master. Characteristically, the Devil's body, and in particular his penis, would be described as being very cold.

Frequently, new converts would be re-named by the Devil. The re-naming could be interpreted as a parody of the Christian ceremony of baptism, or as merely the giving of a secret name by which the individual might be recognised amongst co-participants in witches' meetings. The witches of Auldearn had particularly colourful names, such as 'Pickle Nearest the Wind', and 'Over the Dike with it'. Agnes Sampson, the eldest of the North Berwick coven, told of the protests that arose during the gathering at North Berwick Kirk when the Devil called Robert Grierson by his real name instead of by his nickname, which was 'Robert the Comptroller, *alias* Rob the Rower'.

The Devil could appear in a variety of guises. Sometimes he was said to be in the form of an animal, such as a dog or a cat, or less specifically, a beast. At other times he appeared as a man – he could be young or old, was frequently said to be dressed in black, and most frequently had cloven feet, like a goat.

The Devil in Scotland was not one for solemn ceremony, or Black Mass. Although his meetings with his disciples – sometimes referred to as Sabbats – might take place on consecrated ground, they were not conducted as formal services, it would appear, but as rowdy parties. Often he met with groups of people at someone's home, or an ale-house. Several witch narratives refer to drinking before, or at these meetings. The closest any of the witch meetings on record came to taking the form of a service was at North Berwick, where, as was described at the trial of Agnes Sampson:

John Fian blew up the doors, and blew in the lichts, whilk were like meikle black candles sticking round about the pulpit. The Devil start up himsel in the pulpit, like ane meikle black man, and callit every man by his name, and every ane answerit: "here, Master.". . . The first thing he demandit was, "Gif they had keepit all promise and been good servants?" and "What had they done since the last time they convenit?" On his command, they openit up the graves, twoa within and ane without the kirk, and took off the joints of their fingers, taes and knees, and partit them amang them; and the said Agnes Sampson gat for her part ane winding sheet and twa joints, whilk she tint negligently. The Devil commandit them to keep the joints upon them, while they were dry, and then to make ane powder of them, to do evil withal. Then he commandit them to keep his commandments, whilk were to do all the evil they could.'

When the meeting was over, the witches paid homage to the Devil by kissing him on the bottom.

Witches' confessions commonly referred to feasting, music, dancing, general merriment and a certain amount of lewd behaviour at these occasions. Often it was the Devil who provided the music. Sometimes, it was one of the witches. Geillis Duncan played her jew's harp for the meeting of the witches at North Berwick in 1589. The dances which the witches performed were generally ring-dances, with the participants moving round *widdershins*. Witchcraft narratives frequently refer to witches moving *widdershins* – in the opposite direction to the sun, and hence, contrary to the natural way of things.

But in spite of the revelry, it is clear that there was a certain order about many of these get-togethers. The Devil (or devil figure) was clearly master as well as host, and he gave out his instructions to his servants along with promises of the benefits that could be gained from following his will. From the confessions of some witches, such as Isobel Gowdie and Agnes Sampson, it is apparent that there was a hierarchy within each group of witches. Generally one would take the lead, with one or two others acting as officers. The number of witches in a coven or conventicle varied. Much has been made of the number thirteen, or the 'Devil's Dozen', and some covens – notably that to which Isobel Gowdie of Auldearn belonged – did have thirteen members, but this was not generally the case. Where witches confessed to acting with others, the number of people involved varied considerably.

In addition to coven meetings with the Devil – traditionally held on Hallowe'en, Beltane or other festival days in the calendar, witches would meet their master on other occasions when he had a particular task for them to do. Sometimes, he would be present at and take part in the malicious activities of his proselytes. In the dittay, or indictment of Janet Wishart, who was charged with witchcraft in Aberdeen in 1597, she is accused of having terrified Janet Wood of Pitmurchie and her husband as they lay in their beds at night, shaking the walls of their house at the instigation of the Devil. On the same night, the indictment reads:

'the Devil thy master appeared to thee in the said goodwife of Pitmurchie's chamber, where the goodman himself was lying, in the form of a four-footed beast, and especially like ane futret, and sometime like ane cat, and ran about the said goodman of Pitmurchie's bedclothes where he was lying, whereby he was so terrified that he cried. . .'

The witches generally were told how they could summon their master if they needed him, using a special name, or a phrase that he had bid them repeat. Agnes Finnie of North Berwick used the name 'Elva' to summon the Devil, and Alexander Hamilton of East Lothian had to call out 'Rise up, foul thief!'

Body Parts

There are several references to be found, both in records of witch trials and in legendary tales of witches and warlocks, to the grisly practice of disinterring the corpses of the dead – especially unbaptised infants – for use in witchcraft. The North Berwick witches removed the fingers from corpses buried both within and without the kirkyard. These were to be dried, ground into a powder, and used in spells to kill the king. The Auldearn witches likewise took an unchristened child's body and chopped it up with other distasteful ingredients in a concoction intended to get them corn from Broadley's fields. Helen Guthrie of Forfar, executed for witchcraft in 1661, confessed that she and her fellow witches had made a pie from various parts of the body of an unbaptised child. The eating of this pie was supposed to prevent them from confessing their craft. Clearly, it did not work!

Legendary figures such as Lord Soulis and Alexander Skene were also said to use the corpses of unchristened children for their own ghastly purposes. It is small wonder that new mothers sought to get their children baptised with all due haste, when the possibility of a child's death before baptism risked so much.

Less grisly, but still quite unpleasant, are the common references to fingernails, toenails and hair being used in spells. Hair and nail clippings seem to have had considerable significance both in superstition and practical magic in times gone by.

Transport

> *'We saddled ouir naigis wi' the moon-fern leif,*
> *And rode fra Kilmerrin kirk.*
>
> *Some horses ware of the brume-cow framit,*

> *And some of the greine bay tree;*
> *But mine was made of ane humloke schaw,*
> *And a stout stallion was he.'*

The childhood image of witches riding on broomsticks is not one that is common in the history of Scottish witches, but nevertheless, it seems they had a variety of methods of travelling from place to place. The witches of North Berwick put to sea in sieves, but once on land, seem to have resorted to Shanks's pony, as did many others of their kind. Isobel Gowdie and her cronies could take a couple of straws, and with a cry of 'horse and hattock, in the Devil's name!', could take off into the wide blue yonder, while the witches of Nithsdale had ragweed chariots. Janet Horne of Dornoch was accused of changing her daughter into a magical steed, and there are other references to be found of humans being changed into horses for witches to ride, but there are also accounts of witches having used real horses.

Finally, for speed and effective disguise, what could be better than to transform into a hare, a cat or a bird?

Counter-Charms

There were several different ways of fighting the magic of witchcraft. Sometimes, if a person was believed to have caused harm by a look, a curse, or other magical means, they might be called back to the scene of the 'crime' to see whether any benefit might be achieved. In the case of John Rind from Elgin, we have already seen how his reappearance in the home of the child whom he was believed to have harmed seemed to effect an immediate cure. The suspected harmer might have to be implored to cast another charm, or utter a prayer to undo the harm that they had done. So it was in the case of Christian Shaw of Bargarran. Two of the women whom she accused of troubling her were called upon to pray for her. One of them did so, and troubled her no more. The other refused and continued to torment the girl until taken into custody by the authorities. In other cases where harmful magic was to be reversed, the services of another known witch might be sought. But sometimes, the victims, or those who saw themselves as potential victims, would try to fight back by taking matters into their own hands.

When it was suspected that a witch had been taking milk from a certain cow, for example, there was a specific charm that could be used to get one's revenge. The very last drops of milk had to be squeezed from the cow's udder – this was believed to be bad milk, not fit for drinking – and placed in a pot with a handful of pins. The whole then had to be boiled and stirred over a fire. When this was done, the milk thief would suffer agonising pins and needles all over her body and hopefully would thus be persuaded that the taking of any more milk would be inadvisable.

When someone lay sick and a witch was believed to have cast the evil eye on them, it was believed possible to reverse the ill-effects by 'scoring' the suspect 'above the breath'. 'Scoring above the breath' meant scratching the person, with a blunt instrument, above the nose and mouth – generally on the forehead. The scratch had to be deep enough to draw blood.

Other defences against the effects of an evil eye were described disapprovingly in King James VI's *Daemonologie* as

'such kind of charmes, as commonlie dafte wives uses for healing forspoken goodes, for preserving them from evil eyes, by knitting rountrees or sundriest kind of herbes to the haire and tailes of the goodes'.

There were rhymes, rituals and talismans of all kinds used to counter the effects of harmful magic, but the use of such measures was frowned upon by the church almost as much as black magic. Counter-magic and magical healing were still the Devil's work in the eyes of the clergy. It was all indulgence in 'abominable superstition.'

prove it!

Confession

There were many different means by which suspected witches and warlocks could be proven, at least in the eyes of their interrogators, to be innocent or guilty. The first way to prove a suspect's guilt lay in extracting a confession from the accused. Some of the methods that were used to extract full confessions from those charged with sorcery were particularly cruel, and it is often these upon which some popular accounts of the witch-hunts dwell. It is true that torture was applied – sometimes without legal authority – in many cases, and the extremes of pain and distress that the victims of torture were made to endure were so great that it is small wonder that they gave up confessions, and implicated others in the acts in which they were said to have played a part. 'Thou shalt not suffer a witch to live' was the biblical command. Death must have seemed a blessed release to many. However, not all witches who were brought before their kirk session for investigation were treated in this way. There is no accurate way of telling what percentage of witch investigations used these barbaric methods. Records are incomplete. But it is certain that torture (or the means of applying pain that were at that time defined as torture) was not universal, and in the later years of the witch-hunts, it became illegal.

Nonetheless, the conditions under which the witches were interrogated, and the means by which their confessions were obtained, were of a nature that would never be tolerated in a modern court of law. The sufferings of the accused during the process

Scottish Witches & Wizards

of investigation could sometimes go on for several days – even weeks – while their interrogators worked to persuade them that what had been said of them was true. Sometimes after initial questioning, suspects would be kept in confinement for months while more evidence was gathered against them, before the interrogation started all over again. Although torture as it was then defined was not always used, methods of investigation commonly in practice such as walking and pricking placed the victims under terrible psychological stress and physical discomfort, and the conditions in which the accused were confined – often the local tolbooth – were most likely to be primitive, cold and insanitary. There is no way of telling how many poor souls died from cold, hunger and disease whilst undergoing investigation or awaiting trial, but some inevitably did. The psychological pressures on those who were accused should never be underestimated. From the first moment that suspicion fell on a person's head to the time when enough evidence had been gathered against them to warrant their apprehension, the fear felt by the accused must have been acute. Once apprehended, it was commonly acknowledged that pain and death would be the likely consequences. 'Innocent until proven guilty' was a principle that does not seem to have applied in the case of the witches. The onus was on them to prove their innocence, and all too often they found themselves unable to do so. It is not surprising, under these circumstances, that some suspects were driven to take their own lives.

One example of the kind of treatment accused witches could expect at the hands of their accusers can be found in the records concerning two women from Culross, Mary Cunningham and her daughter Janet Erskine, who were tried by local commission for witchcraft in 1644. Mary Cunningham complained that they were arrested by baillies and taken,

'. . . . *under cloud of night furth of our owne hous, quhilk lyis not within thair jurosdictioune, without any warrand or lawfull authoritie, harling and drawing us throw thair streittes to prisone. . . . and when they had putt us in prisone they causit thair officeris and hangman tirre us mother naked, rype and search our bodies and secreitt memberis for witchmarkis, and when they could find none upon us, they putt on sackcloath gounes upon us and loakit our leggis in yron gaddis and wald suffer nether meatt nor drink to cum in to us bot by the handis of thair jeavellour, wha intercepted the samyne be the way and first satisfied thair owne apietyde thairwith and send in the reversiounes thairof to us, and so throw famyne and cold brought us to great miserie and seiknes.*'

There is no mention of torture as such, but from Margaret Cunningham's statement it is clear that she and her daughter suffered loss of dignity, hunger, cold, discomfort and fear following their arrest. The outcome of their case is not known, but it is more than possible that the two women were executed.

As has been mentioned already, the fact that most of the confessions – even those that were said to have been given 'voluntarily' – were likely to have been elicited under unreasonable duress should give us reason enough to doubt their reliability. The records of some witch trials that are still in existence which give the contents of confessions, particularly those from 1600 onwards, should perhaps give us further reasons for suspicion. Although they might differ in detail, there are often striking similarities in the basic format. First, an account would be given of the accused's first meeting with the Devil. This was followed by a description of the accused's renouncal of baptism, and of the infliction of the Devil's mark. Sometimes, admission of copulation with the Devil would follow this. Subsequent meetings with the Devil were then described, acts of witchcraft were listed, and accomplices were named. The format of these confessions, in fact, closely shadowed the format of the final indictments, which by now had become fairly standardised. The confessions were often closer to the final indictments than the accusations laid against the witches by other people. This can be reasonably assumed to indicate that rather being encouraged to give her own account of her crimes in her own way, the accused had been coerced into admitting the commission of certain key offences, the most important of which was the Demonic Pact, in order to conform to a formula that would ensure a guilty verdict. In other words, the accused, when confessing, had been saying what she was expected, asked, or persuaded to say. Isobel Gowdie's confessions were remarkably long and detailed. But as far as her interrogators were concerned, it would be the key elements in the first confession – the Demonic Pact, the renouncal of baptism, the marking and the naming of others – that counted the most. Perhaps once this information had been elicited from her, her interrogators relaxed, letting her elaborate her story to her heart's content. The rest of her confessions made remarkable listening. They were extravagant in detail. But, from the point of view of the prosecution, they were the icing on the cake. Janet Braidhead's confession, although considerably more sparing with the detail that followed, was strikingly similar in content and form to Isobel's first confession.

Detection – Spot the Witch

Detective work has changed radically over the years. The modern police force make use of computer databases, fingerprint and DNA samples, psychiatrists, psychologists, dentists, doctors, pathologists and forensic scientists and many other resources to help them to identify and track down criminals. Scientific detective work was still a long way off in the sixteenth and seventeenth centuries, but even modern detectives, with access to the services of the most skilled of forensic and other scientists, would find it hard to tell a witch from any other human being without hard evidence (magical paraphernalia, spell books, etc) or a confession.

The witch-hunters of the persecution period did not see witch identification as a problem. They believed it was perfectly possible to identify a witch without the need for any hard evidence, or self-incriminating words on the suspect's part, and they placed great faith in their bizarre methods of detection.

There were three methods of witch identification which might be employed. None of these methods was fair. The first of these was witch-pricking. The second, variations of which were widely used in England and on the Continent, was ordeal by water. The third was ordeal of the bierricht, or ordeal by touch.

Witch-Pricking

The first and most popular method of detecting a witch was by pricking, or 'brodding'. This crude practice, based on widely held beliefs about witches at the time, was humiliating, and no doubt frequently very painful. The theory that lay behind the practice was that all true witches bore, in one or more places about their person, a mark which proved them to be one of the Devil's own – the result of having been touched, kissed or bitten or (according to some) having had their blood sucked by Satan. Such a mark, when pricked, would not bleed, and would be insensible to piercing with a needle. Finding the Devil's mark gave the prosecution proof that a Demonic Pact had taken place. This was the most vital element in pursuing a successful prosecution.

At the height of the witch-hunts in Scotland, witch-pricking became acknowledged as a skill, and several individuals found there was much profit to be gained from the witch-pricking business. It was not only the accusers who might employ the services of a witch-pricker. It happened occasionally that the accused asked for the process to be carried out in an attempt to prove their innocence of the charges against them – but if they did so, they were taking no small risk.

It was believed that the Devil was more likely to leave his mark in a place that was hidden from normal view. Frequently, the mark was found in Scottish witches on the back, between the shoulder blades, but it might also be hidden in the hair, in the eyebrows, or in a more secret place, such as the mouth or on the genitals. Suspected witches were, therefore, quite frequently stripped and shaved in order to facilitate a full inspection. In some cases, the depilation process (and presumably the fear and humiliation that it caused) was enough to elicit an admission of guilt from the accused. But if such an admission was not forthcoming – and it was not in many cases – the presiding officials were then at liberty to begin their search. It took skill to distinguish a satanic mark from a blemish, birthmark or mole and while some witch-finders might profess to be able to make an identification by eye alone, the needle of the witch-pricker was there as insurance. Witch-pricking needles were several inches long and would be driven into the body of the accused wherever the pricker so chose until either an insensible or bloodless spot was found, or the victim, driven to distraction by the torment of the process, offered up a confession.

Janet Cock, a woman from Dalkeith, found herself at the mercy of John Kincaid, from Tranent, one of the most famous witch-prickers of the time. Janet Cock had been accused of witchcraft by some local dignitaries and had also been delated by another woman, Janet Paiston, who had already confessed to her own guilt after similar treatment at Kincaid's hands. In the process of his examination of Janet Cock, John Kincaid found:

'*two marks upon her, and pricked without any sense or feeling thereof,
or any of the least appearance of any blood: the pins being taken out,
the holes remained unclosed, as if the same had been put into white
paper.*'

Janet's fate was sealed and John Kincaid, having successfully
concluded his business, could go home and count his fees. Records
show that six Scots pounds was the going rate; food and drink
were also supplied.

The witch-pricking business was clearly potentially very profit-
able, and it paid the witch-prickers to find their mark. Not surprisingly, therefore, there were some 'brodders' whose methods
were far from fair and some who were eventually exposed as frauds.
John Kincaid had achieved considerable standing as a witch-
pricker, and his services were widely sought, but he was later to
be denounced for having used trickery in his investigations. Several other witch-prickers were also exposed as frauds, but only
after they had been responsible for condemning several souls to
their doom. In 1662, in order to try to stamp out fraud, legisla-
tion was passed in Edinburgh which made it illegal for anyone to
practise witch-pricking without a licence, and towards the end of
the witch-hunts an increasing number of people became dubious
about the real value of the practice, but it continued to be used
until the final years of the period. In the light of modern medical
knowledge it is easy to see the dangers behind the practice, even
if carried out by an honest person, and to recognise that a skilled
witch pricker might be able to find an insensible, bloodless spot
on anyone. It is a sobering thought that the fate of so many individuals rested on this one test, which was held to be valid only
because of the prevalent superstitious beliefs of the time.

Ordeal by Water

Witches, it was believed, did not sink. Another simple method of identifying a witch, therefore, was to try to make the suspect sink in water. Sometimes the accused would merely be thrown into a pool, to see whether she floated or sank. As even drowning people, unless very heavily weighted down, will rise to the surface of the water several times before they sink forever, it is extremely unlikely that any person cast into the water in this manner would be declared innocent. And supposing the accused did sink – or was able to keep herself underwater long enough to convince her accusers she was innocent – how long was long enough? How long before she drowned?

Sometimes the accused would be bound, right hand to left foot and left hand to right foot, before being cast into the pool. Such a position would make it more difficult for the accused to remain afloat. It made her innocence more easily proved but her drowning more likely. Does that make it more cruel or more merciful?

There is little documentary evidence that the ordeal by water was much used in Scotland. There are a number of 'witch pools' around the country, but it is not certain that these pools were so called because witches were ducked in them, or drowned in them. An example of one such pool was the 'Order Pot' of Elgin, a deep pool which once lay on the outskirts of the town, but which is believed to have been filled in some time before the end of the nineteenth century. Its reputation was well-known in the surrounding district, although it is not known whether the stories that were told about it had any basis in fact. One of the stories told of the death of a woman called Marjory Bisset, who had been accused of saying her 'aves' backwards, causing disease in cattle, and changing herself into a hare. There is no record of anyone under that name having been put to death in Elgin for witchcraft, so the story cannot be authenticated, but the tale relates how she was dragged to the pool by angry crowds and thrown in, in spite of her protestations of innocence. She sank beneath the water at first, but then rose again. Her guilt having thereby been 'proved', the crowd were content to let her sink once more and drown. The tale illustrates quite clearly how the logic of the ordeal by water was flawed. Whether or not one is able to swim, it is unlikely that anyone, thrown into deep water, would sink without a struggle. It is not surprising at all that the poor woman rose to the surface for a period of time before the waters finally took her. But the very fact that her reactions were quite normal, in fact, predictable, was enough to convince the watching crowds that she was guilty – and so she was left to her fate. And if she had sunk without a struggle – would they have rescued her?

There are other stories of various 'witch pools' around Scotland, which suggest that pools like this, rather than being places where witches were put to trial, were used as places of execution. One such story comes from the south-west of Scotland; a pitiful tale of a woman whose solitary lifestyle and eccentric behaviour led to a growing suspicion within her own community that she was witch, and should be dealt with accordingly. The story is set in the parish of Irongray, not far from Dumfries, during the reign of James VI but is unauthenticated. According to the story, the local community grew increasingly disturbed by the woman's behaviour and put the clergy under intense pressure to take action against her, in spite of the fact that it had not been proved that she was guilty of any particular malefice. The worst that could be said of her was that she made weather predictions which sometimes came true. At length, the woman was summoned to trial, where it appears that mob rule took over. She was sentenced to be drowned in the burn, but this did not satisfy the assembled crowd's lust for justice as they saw it. They forced the frail body of the poor old soul into a tar-barrel, then set it alight before rolling it into the waters of the river Cluden.

Ordeal of Touch

In a secret Murther, if the dead carkasse bee at any time thereafter handled by the Murtherer, it will gush out of blood; as if the blood were crying to the heaven for revenge of the Murtherer, God having appointed that secret supernaturall trial of that sectre unnaturall crime.

King James VI, *Daemonologie*.

> *'The maiden touched the clay-cold corpse,*
> *A drop it never bled;*
> *The Lady laid her hand on him*
> *And soon the ground was red.'*

The Ballad of Earl Richard

It was quite common for a 'witch' to be accused of having caused the death of someone through magic – by giving them the 'evil eye', by having cursed them, or by having performed a spell to bring about their death. In a few of these cases, the accused was made to undergo the ordeal of touch. This was a practice which was also occasionally used to identify the guilty party in a murder case where no witchcraft was suspected. The accused would be taken to the dead body of the victim and made to touch it in the presence of witnesses. If the body bled, then guilt was considered proven. In order for this ordeal to be possible, of course, there would have to be a fresh corpse, and this was not always possible. There is little to suggest that it was commonly practised, but there are one or two examples to be found in existing records of cases relating to witchcraft. Christian Wilson of Dalkeith, who was delated as a witch in 1661, was made to undergo an ordeal of touch. She had been accused of causing the death of her own brother, Alexander Wilson, following a dispute with him. The enmity between the two siblings was well-known, and when Alexander Wilson was found dead one day, with the cause of death unknown, Christian, who already had a reputation as a witch, was summoned and made to touch the body of her brother. When she touched the corpse, blood began to run from a fresh cut on his face, and Christian's fate was effectively sealed. Christian was one of a group of five witches who were executed together.

Walking

Walking, watching, or waking an accused witch was common practice. It was not recognised as torture in the days of the witch-hunts, but nowadays it is acknowledged to be a particularly inhumane practice, despite the fact that, because of its undoubted effectiveness in breaking the spirit of the victim, it is sadly still used on prisoners in some parts of the world.

Witches, it was believed, did not need to sleep, and so they were kept from rest for considerable periods of time during investigations. Sleep deprivation is hard for anyone to bear. Its effects on both the body and the psyche can be quite profound. When the body of a person in a state of fatigue seeks the rest it requires and the person starts to fall asleep involuntarily, it becomes progressively harder to enforce and maintain wakefulness. Continuing fatigue causes increasing distress, physical pain, and mental confusion. Hallucinations are commonly experienced by people who are seriously sleep deprived. Driven half-mad with fatigue – and the physical pain which the fatigue also caused – it is hardly surprising that many witches came out with the confessions

67

that were asked of them after a period of walking. How many of the confessions sprang directly from hallucinations? It is impossible to tell.

Sometimes a particularly cruel device known as a 'witch's bridle' was used in order to keep the tormented captive awake. There are one or two examples of this still in existence today. The witch's bridle was made of metal, and consisted of a band designed to fit over the head of the victim from front to back, attached to another band, which curved round the back and sides of the head. To this band was attached a mouthpiece; four metal spikes which would be forced into the victim's mouth, one pointing to the roof of the mouth, one pointing downwards, and the other two pointing to the sides, into the cheeks. The bridle would be fixed round the victim's head and padlocked at the front. Unable to speak, swallow, or move her tongue without considerable pain, the victim might be kept in this fiendish device for several hours at a time.

Torture

Given that most of the victims were women, many of whom were elderly, and that all of those who officiated at or took part in extracting confessions from so-called witches were men, the barbarity of these practices is particularly breathtaking. The torturers had a choice of several methods from which they could choose and time, it would appear, was on their side. They could go on for as long as they chose, until they had gathered from their victim a long enough list of 'accomplices' and a satisfactory account of all diabolical practices in which their victim would admit to having taken part.

Although at the time it was given little, if any consideration, mental torture was inevitable. The fear of their captors, of the pain that might be inflicted and the death which probably awaited at the end of their ordeal, would dominate every waking moment.

Sometimes a more sinister pressure was put upon the victim. The interrogators did not always confine themselves to inflicting pain upon the accused alone. It happened on occasion that members of the family of the accused were brought into custody and put through agonies within sight of him or her. This was what happened in the case of Alison Balfour, of Orkney, who was burned at the stake in 1594. Her tormentors had tortured her for some forty-eight hours and had failed to extract a confession from her, so they brought in her elderly husband, her son and her seven-year-old daughter and subjected them to torture before her eyes. Seeing her loved ones in tremendous pain was more than the poor woman could bear, and, quite naturally, she offered up the confession that was desired to her. As a result of this, she was sentenced to death. On her way to her execution however, she retracted her confession, telling all those who might listen of the ordeals that she and her family had been put through. She went to her death boldly maintaining her innocence of all charges and asking God's forgiveness for having confessed.

Various devices were used to inflict pain. The caschielaws, in which Alison Balfour of Orkney suffered and was

'sundry times taken out of them dead, and out of all remembrance either of good or evil',

is thought to have been a device in which the victim's legs were placed before either weights were placed on top to crush the legs, or screws were tightened to obtain similar results.

The boot, or bootikin (a name that sounds eerily endearing) was a similar device. It consisted of a wooden case in which one

69

of the victim's legs was placed. Wedges were driven into either end of the boot, causing agonising pain and terrible deforming injuries. Whether found guilty or innocent, it is unlikely that anyone ever walked away from the boot.

Another common device of torture was a form of thumbscrew, variously called the thumbikins, pilliewinks and pilniewinks. Tightening the screws on these ingeniously compact devices caused excruciating pain to the person whose thumbs had been placed therein.

If none of the above was available for use, the torturers still had several tricks up their sleeves. The victim's fingernails might be ripped out with pincers (turkas) or have pins driven beneath them. Burning was also used as a method of torture, commonly on the tender soles of the feet, but also on other parts of the anatomy. The victim might be suspended from the roof with heavy weights attached to the feet, which would stretch the muscles and ligaments agonisingly. Or the victim's head might be 'thrawn' with a knotted rope, twisted round it until unbearably tight, and then pulled and jerked from side to side to twist the neck and further pain the victim.

There was little chance that anyone subjected to one or a variety of the above treatments would be able to withstand the pain for any great length of time and yet, surprisingly, some individuals did manage to hold out for considerable periods of torture. The case of Dr Fian, accused as one of the leaders of the witches in North Berwick, is described with bloodthirsty relish in *Newes from Scotland*. He was apprehended and tortured until he confessed to the crimes of which he had been accused, but then somehow managed to escape. He was recaptured and, as he claimed that his first confession had been false and made under extreme duress, he was subjected to further tortures. This time, we are told:

His nailes upon all his fingers were riven and pulled off with an instrument called in Scottish a Turkas, which in England wee call a payre of pincers, and under everie nayle there was thrust in two needels over even up to the heads. At all which tormentes notwithstanding, the Doctor never shronke anie whit; neither would he then confesse it the sooner, for all the tortures inflicted upon him. Then was hee, with all convenient speede, by commandement, convaied againe to the torment of the bootes, wherein hee continued a long time, and did abide so many blowes in them, that his legges were crusht and beaten together as small as might bee; and the bones and flesh so brused, that the bloud and marrow spouted forth in great abundance; whereby they were made unserviceable for ever.

Dr Fian still refused to confess again, in spite of the best (or worst) efforts of his tormentors. His claims of innocence fell on deaf ears. The testimonies of his co-accused, his reputation as a magician, and his original confession were enough. He was condemned to death, strangled and burnt.

Reputation

'See that ye say not that I have bewitched you, as other neighbours say'

Agnes Finnie, Edinburgh

'Isobel McGown in Netherton, who being called and compearing, declares that Jean McMurrie has been under the name of a witch for many years by the report of the country.'

Trial of Jean McMurrie, Twynholm 1703

Although the term 'witch' is not one commonly used in the modern repertoire of insults, if and when it is used, it is most unlikely to carry anything like the same weight as it did four hundred years ago. Reputation counted for a great deal in the sixteenth and seventeenth centuries, both in the courts and in the wider community. To be secretly suspected of being a witch was bad enough; to be widely acknowledged as one was worse, and to be openly accused of being one was downright dangerous. Nowadays, when someone is charged with murder, or theft, there is visible and/or tangible evidence that a such crime has been committed; moreover, there is generally visible and tangible evidence that the person charged could reasonably be presumed to be involved. As has already been mentioned, charges of witchcraft were not generally founded on the same sort of evidence. They were all too frequently dependent upon the word of one or more people against another. The evidence did not have to be tangible or visible – it was frequently little more than hearsay. Thus, to call someone a witch was more than name-calling; it could be life-threatening.

Nowadays, if a person appears in court charged with a serious offence, and has previous convictions for similar offences, it is unlikely, except in exceptional circumstances, that the jury will be made aware of that person's previous convictions (and hence his or her character and reputation) during the trial procedure, lest it sway them in their verdict. Whilst a judge may take previous convictions into account when considering sentence, the jury's job is to consider whether the accused is innocent or guilty in the light of the evidence relating to the crime of which he stands accused, and not in the light of his character or previous convictions. Very often the charges laid against people suspected of witchcraft in the period of the witch-hunts included phrases such as 'by habit and repute a witch', or 'of ill-fame'.

Although it would not stand by itself as proof of guilt, the reputation and character – or perceived character – of the accused counted for a great deal.

It is clear from the existing records of witch trials that many of the men and women who were accused were permitted to live in their communities unharmed for several years, in spite of being suspected of being, or even accepted as being, practicioners of sorcery. This was especially true of the healers. From court and kirk session records, we can see that several of those who were tried and found guilty had been practising their healing art, and had even been sought out for their skills, for some years before they were finally apprehended. Eventually, something – it might be failure to effect a cure, suspected harm, dispute, or witch-hatred – led to accusations finally being made to the kirk session, and reputation became incriminating evidence.

In the event that a person who had been accused of witchcraft was set free, or was among those who were fortunate to escape the death sentence, it was all too often the case that their reputation, even if the case had been found not proven or they had been found not guilty, was enough to blight their lives permanently.

In 1650, Janet Anderson of Aberdour was apprehended, accused of witchcraft. Records show that she was kept in custody while a witch-pricker was summoned. She must have secured her release, but she clearly did not lose her reputation, because records show that several years after the event, she wished to move out of the parish and applied to the kirk session for a 'testimonial'. The kirk session duly obliged, but were careful to mention the fact that she had been accused of being a witch. Janet Anderson might be able to leave the parish, but she could certainly not leave her past behind. And with a testimonial such as this, it is unlikely that she would find acceptance anywhere else.

Beatrix Laing of Pittenweem, accused of witchcraft in 1704,

but eventually released on payment of a fine, found herself an outcast from her own village, forced into a life of vagrancy, on account of her now established reputation.

The label 'witch' was taken so seriously that name-calling incidents frequently resulted in complaints of slander. One of several entries referring to slander, that can be found in kirk session records from various parts of Scotland, comes from the parish of Irongray in the south-west:

> *'David Muirhead of Drumpark and his wife, being called before the Session and examined anent the strife betwixt them and Janet Sinklar, submitted themselves to the will of the Session. Janet Sinklar also submitted to the will of the Session for saying that she doubted Drumpark's wife of murder and witchcraft, and is appointed to receive publik rebuke before the congregation.'*

The words of Agnes Finnie (above) give some indication of the fear that people had of being called a witch. 'Witch' was a label that stuck, and for many of those who were made to wear it, it might as well have said 'Here I am – come and get me.'

Evidence

Once a formal accusation of witchcraft had reached the ears of the kirk session, it was their job to look for evidence to make a case against the accused, before making application for a commission to try the accused locally, or for trial at the High Court. Information from people who were familiar with the accused – neighbours, sometimes friends, relatives – was eagerly gathered by the church authorities. In cases where two or more witches had fallen under suspicion, each of the accused was encouraged (or forced) to implicate the others.

Whilst in some cases, those accused had been self-acknowledged practising witches, in other cases it was what was generally believed of them, rather than what they could be proved to have done. As has been mentioned before, it was all too often the case that two and two were put together to make five. A few harsh words said by someone in anger, combined with unfortunate coincidence, moved people towards the conclusion that that person was a witch. When similar scenarios were repeated on more than one occasion, or were remembered to have happened before, the danger for that person increased. Once a complaint had been made to the kirk session, it was only a matter of finding enough people who had stories like this to make the court convinced of the accused's guilt. None of the stories would be accepted in a modern court of law as evidence of guilt. There might have been misfortune, but there was no real physical evidence that the cause had to be witchcraft. There might have been threats, but there was no 'smoking gun' to incriminate the accused. What counted as acceptable evidence of guilt in the witchcraft trials of sixteenth and seventeenth century Scotland was often little more than a collection of ill-founded suspicions.

The evidence against Jean McMurrie of Twynholm, Dumfriesshire, who was investigated by the kirk session in 1703 for witchcraft, typifies this sort of case.

It is clear that Jean was not popular in her parish, and her reputation as a witch, probably founded on one whispered rumour which had grown over the years, was long-standing. At least three people gave testimony to the kirk session that she had been

'under the name of a witch by report of the country.'

Jean clearly had a temper – whether her reputation as a witch was initially founded upon episodes when she had displayed ill-temper, or whether her ill-temper was a result of her harsh treatment by others who knew of her reputation, is hard to tell. But the kirk session was furnished with no less than five testimonies telling of incidents when Jean's anger had been aroused. Following these angry episodes, according to the testimonies, the people who were the objects of her anger suffered misfortune of some sort.

Jean had asked one man, Thomas Craig, for some meat, but he had refused her and Jean had stormed off in a rage, cursing Thomas and his wife. Approximately one week later, one of Thomas's calves drowned. On another occasion, Jean had become angry when John Neilson had refused to pay the price she was asking for some corn. Shortly after Neilson had this angry exchange of words with Jean, his horse died.

The other three stories were similar. In each case, Jean wanted something, was refused, lost her temper, and within a short space of time something unpleasant happened to the person with whom she had been angry.

Jean McMurrie was relatively fortunate. These incidents happened in 1703, a time when the witch-frenzy in Scotland was dying down. No comission was sought to try her. Instead, she was banished from the district. But her case demonstrates the nature of evidence that was built up around many of those who were delated of witchcraft. In a period of history when medicine was in its infancy and little was known about disease, people frequently believed illness in humans and animals to have preternatural causes and looked around for someone to blame for having brought about their misfortune in this way. Thus, the presence of a person in the district with a reputation as a malefactor or a healer (for healers had the potential to do harm), curses spoken by that person in anger (whether these were intentional curses or hasty words did not matter) and coincidental unpleasant occurrences such as injury, disease or death, were factors that were common to many witch prosecutions. The evidence against Jean

McMurrie was, at best, circumstantial; it was hardly even that. But it was typical of much of the evidence that was gathered against witches all over Scotland and used against them in their trials.

In multiple witch trials, such as those of the Auldearn and North Berwick witches, the testimony of one accused against another played an important role. Thus, when the first of the North Berwick witches to come under suspicion, Geillis Duncan, was interrogated, her confession implicated several others and they, in turn, added to the number of accusations with their own testimonies. Isobel Gowdie of Auldearn, whose extravagant confessions have earned her particular notoriety, named the twelve other people in her coven.

As has been mentioned already, there were particular reasons to doubt this sort of evidence. It came from those who had already been persuaded to confess their own guilt, and whether the confession had been obtained under torture or not, the accused would most likely have suffered, at least, considerable discomfort and fear. Having admitted their own guilt, and thus having virtually signed their own death warrant, the confessor would have nothing to lose by giving up the names of others and, in all likelihood, would have something to gain – the release from further exhausting and perhaps painful interrogation. The chance to implicate others might also be an opportunity for revenge, if any was sought.

In some witchcraft cases, another kind of evidence was used against the accused. Visible manifestation of the detrimental effects that the alleged malefice of the accused was believed to have had, and continued to have, on their victim's wellbeing. A classic example of this kind of evidence can be found in the case of Christian Shaw of Bargarran, who accused a number of people of causing her harm through witchcraft. She displayed an astonishing variety of symptoms, including pains, fits, loss of consciousness and paralysis, as long as her alleged tormentors remained at large. When all those whom she accused had been dealt with appropriately, she regained her health.

The case of the schoolmaster John Fian, a leading figure in the witches of North Berwick, is another example. He was alleged to have caused daily fits of madness in one of his victims. James VI expressed an interest in seeing this remarkable phenomenon for himself. The man was brought before the King and obliged with a convincing display. We might object to the reliability of this sort of evidence and call it hysteria, or fraud, but in the days of the witch-hunts, it was more likely to be taken seriously and used to push the suspect one step nearer to the flames.

Accusations of causing harm, stories of curses followed by misfortunes and hysterical displays by alleged victims might also serve another purpose in those cases where the accused had uttered curses, or practised witchcraft. They might convince the accused that their magic was effective. If they believed this, then it is quite conceivable that they might be more willing to admit their guilt.

Escape from the Flames

When a woman or man was delated and apprehended as a witch in the sixteenth or seventeenth centuries in Scotland, the most frequent outcome was a guilty verdict. Trial in the High Court gave more favourable odds for acquittal, but most witch trials were carried out by local commission and there, the statistics were bleaker. There were few escape routes for those accused. For the richer and more influential people, the outlook was a little more optimistic. They could arm themselves with powerful legal representation, or use their position and influence in society to their own benefit. So it was that Lady Foulis and her stepson Hector Munro were set at liberty in 1590, when other less influential accomplices in their malevolent practices had already gone to the stake. But for those who did not have the money or the power – and these were in the majority – the opportunities to walk free from an accusation of witchcraft were rare.

Some people did not wait for accusations that had been made against them to reach the ears of the kirk session. By the time a warrant for their arrest had gone out, they had fled the district, believing it was better to run than face the consequences of an interrogation. Of course, not all these bids for freedom were successful; the suspects were frequently hunted down and brought back to face justice.

Occasionally, matters were dealt with at the level of the kirk session, and the accused would be spared a trial. This might be because the evidence against the accused was too slight to warrant application for a commission, or because the offences that they were alleged to have committed were not of such a serious nature as those of which others had been found guilty. Undoubtedly, some kirk sessions would be more inclined to lenience than others. In some cases therefore, the good men of the church might consider that public penance or banishment – sometimes acquittal – was justice enough, and the accused was spared. But even if a person accused of witchcraft did manage to avoid trial on one occasion, reputation, as has already been mentioned, counted for a great deal. Life after accusation, whether successful or otherwise, could be very difficult. Additional accusations, necessitating further investigation, often followed by prosecution, were also quite possible.

As has been mentioned already, it was sometimes possible for a woman or man who had been called a witch, or delated as a witch, to contest the name-calling, or charges made against him or her, with a successful counter-accusation of slander. Slander was treated quite seriously by the kirk sessions and someone found guilty of the offence would be likely to face public and sometimes painful humiliation. A counter-accusation made before a suspected witch was summoned by the kirk session, if successful, would stop the accusers in their tracks, for the meantime at least. Successful counter-accusations after the investigation process had begun had to be made quite swiftly, if they were to succeed; before the weight of evidence accumulating against the accused became too heavy to ignore.

Once an accused witch had been apprehended, release was still possible. Sometimes proceedings came to a halt after the Privy Council or the High Court decided that the case against the accused was not strong enough to go ahead. In the period of the Protectorate, and in the later years of the witch-hunts, this happened more frequently. And two more possibilities presented themselves as means of avoiding the fate which lay at the end of the judicial process. One was escape, the other was death.

There were no buildings specifically designed to keep prisoners securely locked up for considerable lengths of time in sixteenth century Scotland. Justice was generally swiftly dealt, and sentences – whatever the crime – did not include long terms in prison. When a person was accused of witchcraft, they would most likely be kept in the local tolbooth, if there was one, or in the church steeple, under the watchful eye of certain appointed people. But places such as these were not particularly secure; nor could the vigilance or trustworthiness of the watchers always be relied upon, and from time to time, escapes happened. Even John Fian, accused not just of witchcraft but also of treason in 1591, although eventually recaptured, was allowed to escape from captivity in Edinburgh. Where escape was possible, and successfully accomplished, the fugitive still faced tremendous hardship, forced into a life of vagrancy, trying to keep body and soul together whilst hiding from justice. Diligent efforts would be made to find the escapee, and these were quite often successful. Nor did time allow people to forget. A woman called Janet McNicol was apprehended on the Isle of Bute in 1662, accused of being a witch. She managed to flee and remained at liberty for eleven years. Unfortunately, when she returned to Rothesay in 1673, she found that justice had a long memory. She was tried, found guilty, strangled and burned.

If escape proved impossible, the other way in which justice might be avoided at this stage in the process was through death – either illness or suicide. The former would quite likely have been caused by the conditions under which the accused was held, and there are a number of references in existing records to the deprivations and ill treatment suffered by accused witches whilst in captivity. Suicide attempts were relatively frequent, and understandable in the light of what the captives endured and still had to face. Some attempts succeeded. If a suicide attempt succeeded, it sometimes happened that the witch's prosecutors saw fit to pursue the course of justice to its proper end regardless. The same applied if a convicted or accused witch died from other causes before her execution. For example, in Ayr in 1650, a woman called Janet Smellie died in the tolbooth whilst awaiting trial for withcraft. Her guilt was presumably not in question, for rather than being given a decent burial, the following order was issued:

'. . . *with the advyse of Mr Robert Adair, minister ordine. . . . that her corpses sall be drawn upon ane slaid to the gallows foot and burnt in ashes.*'

Ayrshire saw the burning of several witches that year. Twelve were burned at once in Irvine. In the light of this, it is not hard to imagine the frustration of the authorities at the thought that one might have 'got away'.

The last glimmers of light for an accused witch during the trial process were to be found in the possibility of leniency, an acquittal, or the hope that an appeal might prove successful. Both successful appeals and acquittals became more frequent in the final years of the seventeenth century. An appeal might be made by relatives of the accused or by a lawyer. If it was successful, the accused might secure his or her release. If unsuccessful, the time taken for an appeal had at least the (dubious) merit of delaying the trial process. Leniency was the third hope, and those who were shown it escaped the death penalty, and were sentenced to banishment, branding – both of which were painful alternatives in different ways – or, occasionally, a caution with public penance.

It was possible to avoid the rope and the flames, and many did, even if they only did so by dying. Nonetheless, for the majority of accused witches, the outlook was grim during the period of the witch-hunts. And for those who escaped the flames, the threat of further torment frequently hung over them for the rest of their lives.

The Sentence

Although it could take quite a long period from initial apprehension to trial, once the trial of a witch had come to its conclusion and the terrible sentence had been pronounced, it was generally carried out quite promptly. There was therefore little time for family or legal representation (if the accused had any) to appeal against the sentence. Although a few more fortunate souls (most of whom were found guilty of witchcraft in the final years of the witch persecutions) escaped capital punishment and were sentenced instead to banishment, most were condemned to death, most commonly to be 'wirriet' – strangled at the stake (although sometimes the victim was hung on the gallows), and burned –

commonly in a tar-barrel. The strangling did not necessarily kill the victim. Sometimes alleged witches were not dead, but unconscious when consigned to the fire. Executions were public affairs, and would be well-attended, in spite of the fact that they must have been horrific occasions. In Aberdeen, a palisade had to be built to restrain the crowds who gathered to watch several witch executions in 1597.

Sometimes, thankfully rarely, witches were 'burnt quick', that is, burned alive. This was the fate of Euphame Macalyean of the North Berwick witches; presumably, it was thought that her crimes were worse than those of her co-accused and that she deserved this particularly agonising and barbaric end. Some witches in Brechin suffered similarly in 1608 and a report of the terrible affair tells the reader how the women screamed and swore as the flames took them. Some managed to break free and stagger out of the fire 'half brunt', only to be thrown back in again. The cruelty of a spectacle such as this is unimaginable.

The Cost

There was no profit to be made by the local parish from witch trials – indeed, the whole process could turn out to be remarkably costly. When a person had been found guilty of witchcraft, it was accepted practice that all their goods were forfeited to the Crown. The parish might extract some funds from this for its own expenses, but was unlikely to recoup the full cost. Sometimes the surviving family of the accused were ordered to contribute towards the cost of the execution, which seems exceptionally harsh. In the majority of witch trials, most of the financial responsibility for arresting, confining, interrogating, trying and executing witches fell to the parishes, and in those areas where the witch count was higher than average, it is a sign of the dogged determination of the authorities to root out the evildoers amongst their midst that they did not flinch in facing up to their responsibilities, for the trials cost them dear.

The accused had to be confined during the investigation process. This would involve the supply of food and drink for the accused and those who acted as jailors. The jailors would also require a fee. Sometimes, the investigations dragged on for months, so this could entail considerable expense. If the services of a pricker were called upon, he would be paid handsomely for his efforts. When the kirk session eventually decided to apply for a commission, someone would have to be paid to travel to Edinburgh with the papers. The commission itself entailed another fee. Finally, if the trial resulted in a guilty verdict and a sentence of death, a cart and driver would be required to take the condemned to the site of execution. Then the services of a hangman would be required, and he would need refreshments and payment. On top of all that had to be added the cost of rope for the hanging or strangling, and coal and tar for the burning. When Janet Wishart and Isobel Cockie were strangled and burnt in 1597 in Aberdeen, the costs of their execution included:

Twenty loads of peat: Forty shillings
One boll of coals: Twenty three shillings
Four tar-barrels: twenty six shillings
Fire and iron barrels: sixteen shillings and eightpence
Buying and dressing a stake: sixteen shillings
Ropes: four shillings
Carriage of equipment to place of execution: thirteen shillings and fourpence
Executioner's fee: thirteen shilings and fourpence.

Scrupulous recording of the expenses incurred in the trial of

Elspeth McEwen, who was burned in Kirkcudbright in 1698, include the purchase of one and a half pounds of candle for the night of the assize, drinks for the Provost on the day of the execution, the services of a drummer to beat his drum at the execution and a full set of clothes for the executioner, William Kirk.

the guilty ones: famous witch trials

Bessie Dunlop of Ayrshire

The case of Bessie Dunlop dates from 1576, thirteen years after the witchcraft act was passed in Scotland. It is a sad tale of an unhappy woman who lived a hard life and suffered a cruel death for alleged crimes that in all likelihood harmed nobody and perhaps helped some. Bessie Dunlop was a married woman, the wife of Andrew Jack from Lyne in Ayrshire. She was apprehended in September 1576 and brought to trial in November. Bessie had a longstanding reputation as a healer, and had also been asked by several individuals for help in finding stolen goods, a skill for which she was well-known, over the years. The charges against her reflect the fact that her reputation had been established over time. She was charged with:

'the using of Sorcerie, Witchcraft and Incantatione, with invocation of spretis of the devill, continewand in familiaritie with thame, at all sic tymes as sche thocht expedient, deling with charmes, and abusingthe pepill with devillisch craft of sorcerie foirsaid. . . usit thie divers yeiris bypast'.

The phrase 'invocation of spretis of the devill' specifically relates to the manner in which Bessie Dunlop told her interrogators she came about her knowledge of healing. Bessie claimed she was given information by the spirit of an old man called Thomas Reid, who had died at the Battle of Pinkie.

Some years before, Bessie said, she had found herself in a state of considerable distress and misery. Her husband lay sick in bed, one of her cows was dead and another was ailing, and she had recently given birth to a child who was clearly not thriving. She was driving her cows to pasture when an old man appeared before her and greeted her in a friendly fashion. He was dressed in a grey coat and grey breeches, with white stockings. He wore a black bonnet on his head and carried a white stick. The old man had asked why Bessie was so upset and she told him of her troubles. His reply to her did not bring much comfort, for he told her that her child would die, as would the sick cow and two of her sheep. However, Bessie was given some hope, for the old man said that her husband would recover. Having told her this, the old man disappeared through a hole in the wall, too small for any earthly man to pass through.

The meeting was the first of several. When Bessie voiced doubts about who Thomas Reid was, he gave her information about his surviving family. His son Thomas worked for the Laird of Blair, and Thomas the elder had encouraged Bessie to speak with him, to confirm the truth about him, and also to pass on a message from the dead father to his son.

Over the coming years, Thomas Reid helped Bessie many times. When someone was sick, Bessie could ask Thomas what the matter was, and he would tell her, giving her recipes, and sometimes the ingredients of herbal medicines and salves that she could use to bring about a cure. When someone asked her about stolen or missing property, Bessie would ask Thomas for the information that she needed and he would supply it.

There was no mention of the Devil, or a Demonic Pact. Thomas, Bessie said, had asked her on two occasions to accompany him to Elfhame (the fairy kingdom), but she had refused. On one occasion, Bessie had been visited by a mysterious woman who Thomas later told her was his mistress, the Queen of Elfhame. Bessie had also seen several members of the fairy folk – once, with Thomas, in the kailyard beside her own home, once when they appeared as a company of riders thundering into the waters of Restalrig Loch, near Leith, and on at least one other occasion.

Whoever, or whatever, Thomas was – hallucination, vision, or perhaps a real man – it appears that Bessie grew quite comfortable with his appearances to her. She accepted that it was only with his guidance that she was able to heal the sick and find missing goods. She adamantly denied having any knowledge of any sort that might allow her to do anything like that unaided. It was also clear that Thomas could be seen only by Bessie, even if he appeared to her when she was in the company of others. When Thomas had come to her home one day, Bessie's husband and some of his friends had been present in the house, but as Thomas drew Bessie out of the house and into the kailyard, the others in the company remained oblivious to his presence. Robert Chambers, writing in his *Domestic Annals of Scotland*, seems to have been in no doubt about the case of Bessie Dunlop. He wrote: 'The modern student of insanity can have no difficulty with this case: it is simply one of hallucination, the consequence of diseased conditions.' But others might not be so certain that the explanation of Bessie's case is as simple as that. Certainly, Thomas Reid appeared to her at a particularly vulnerable moment in her life. Her child was mortally sick, her husband ill also. Her animals were poorly – some of them dying – and so her livelihood was threatened. She herself had recently given birth and would be weak in body and frail in mind – perhaps even suffering from post-partum depression. But Thomas Reid continued to appear to Bessie long after this, and if she was insane, we cannot ignore the fact that there were obviously many other people who were prepared to buy into her insanity, to believe in what she could achieve on their behalf with the help of Thomas. Her reputation for being able to do the things that she could do was only able to grow because other people continued to allow her, and ask her to do them.

Bessie Dunlop had no accomplices; she was not part of any devilish coven, meeting in the dead of night to perform secret rites. Apart from consulting with Thomas Reid, she worked alone. Moreover, there is no mention of her intending harm to anyone. It seems that every time she sought the advice of the mysterious Thomas, she did so in order to be of assistance to others. She cured sick people and sick animals alike:

'She mendit John Jack's bairn, and Wilson's of the town, and her gudeman's sister's cow.'

Bessie Dunlop's services were called upon by many different people, not only those from her own lowly class in society:

'The Lady Thirdpart in the barony of Renfrew sent to her and speerit at her, wha was it that had stolen frae her twa horns of gold, and ane crown of the sun, out of her purse. And after she had spoken with Tom, within twenty days, she sent her word wha had them; and she gat them again.'

Bessie also helped Lady Blair locate some stolen clothes.

It is unclear what finally caused Bessie to be apprehended and questioned. Certainly, her reputation as a healer was well-known, but from details of her interrogation, it is hard to imagine that her apprehension was the result of any claims of malefice against others, as was most often the case in witch trials. It seems more likely that Bessie was the victim of a change of attitude that was gradually taking hold of the country in the post-Reformation years. She was able to effect cures, but admitted she herself did not know how they worked. The cures, therefore, had to be the practice of witchcraft. She communicated with some sort of spirit, or apparition. This spirit had to be the Devil, or associated with him, for no such phenomenon could be associated with God's work. Although Bessie specifically denied that she had renounced her baptism or willingly acted in the service of the Devil, her denial counted for nothing.

In theory, all those who had used the services of Bessie Dunlop should have been apprehended as well. If she was practising witchcraft then they, as consulters, were also guilty of a crime. This did not happen. The jury found Bessie Dunlop guilty of all the charges against her, and she was condemned to death.

Katherine Ross, Lady Foulis

Katherine Ross, the daughter of Alexander Ross of Balnagowan, was the second wife of Robert Munro, the fifteenth baron of Foulis and chief of the clan Munro. Her husband had five children by his first marriage, the eldest of whom, Robert, found himself in ill-favour with his stepmother. Katherine's dislike of Robert moved her to hatch an ingenious plan in order to dispose of him, making Hector, the second eldest, heir to his father. In addition to her murderous designs on Robert, Katherine also had plans for his widow. She intended Robert's widow to become the wife of her brother George Ross – the only obstacle to achieving this being George's wife, whom Katharine also planned to dispose of. Her willing accomplice in these plans was Hector, who stood to benefit greatly from his older brother's death.

Katherine's murderous intentions were first put into action in

1577, but her first attempt at getting rid of her victims, using rat poison, resulted in failure. Lady Balnagowan swallowed some of the contaminated food, but the dose of poison it contained was not enough to kill her. She fell ill, but subsequently recovered. Two separate attempts to take poison to Robert's house met with disaster. On the first occasion, the jar was dropped and the carrier, a nurse from Katherine's household, died after tasting what spilled out. On the second occasion, a servant boy licked some leakage from the jar off his fingers and was taken ill. But Robert remained unharmed.

Katherine was determined to succeed. She had already consulted witches in order to determine whether her plan was likely to succeed, and had called upon the services of a reputed witch called Marjorie MacAlasdair (alias Lasky Loncart) and a warlock by the name of William MacGillivray to help her with her poison plot. Now she turned to magic for more help. She took further advice and help from Lasky Loncart, and two other known witches, Christian Malcolmson and Thomas McKane. With her three accomplices, Katherine fashioned a figure of her youngest stepson out of butter and tried to shoot at it with elf-darts. Their attempts to shoot the butter figure were in vain and so they then made a second figure out of clay, but once more their shots failed to hit the mark. Undeterred, Katherine continued trying in the coming weeks, assisted by Lasky Loncart, Christian Malcolmson, Thomas McKane, Agnes Roy and William MacGillivray (either together or individually), to cause the deaths of Robert and her sister-in-law with poison and figure magic. She may have involved others in her endeavours. Although her efforts were in vain, they must have attracted the attention of others – including her own family. Katherine's husband obtained a commission to try thirty-one suspected witches from Ross, Ardnamurchan and Inverness in 1578. All of those whom Katherine had called upon for help were eventually arrested. They were all found guilty and sentenced to death.

At this point, Katherine took fright, and fearing for her own life, fled to the sanctuary of the home of her uncle, the Earl of Caithness. She stayed there for nine months or so, returning to her husband only when she felt it was safe to do so. All went quiet for a considerable period of time. Then, ten years later, Katherine's husband died and young Robert succeeded him. Robert was not willing to forgive and forget, it would appear, for in 1588 he obtained a commission to try several witches. His timing was bad, and political upheavals of the time (the revolt of the Catholic Earls) gave Katherine the opportunity to obtain a postponement. Nonetheless, in 1590, she was finally summoned for trial. Hector, who had known of her activities and given his blessing – perhaps assisted her – all along, was appointed to the commission. Although ten years before he had been happy to conspire with Katherine, he had had a change of heart, and the two had become enemies.

Katherine denied all the charges against her, and in spite of the fact that her name had been mentioned several times in the trials of her witch accomplices in 1578, she was found not guilty. Perhaps the make-up of the jury, many of whom had surnames Ross or Munro, had something to do with it. This factor, combined with the fact that she was a figure of considerable influence, undoubtedly swayed the verdict.

Shortly after Katherine's trial, Hector himself was brought before the court. He had escaped any implication in Katherine's activities, but he was accused of having used witchcraft on two separate occasions in 1588 and 1589. On the first occasion, he had used the services of two witches to try to cure his brother Robert – the same brother whom he would have been happy to see dead ten years before. Then one year later, Hector himself had fallen ill, and had called upon a witch by the name of Marion MacIngaroch. Marion had told him that the only way he could be cured was if another person was to die in his place. Hector agreed, choosing George, Katherine's own son by Robert Munro, as the person whom he wished to die instead of himself. Hector took part in a series of bizarre magical rituals over a period of several days under the guidance of Marion and another woman called Christian Ross. He recovered from his illness, and five months later, his step-brother George died after a brief illness.

Hector, like his wicked stepmother, was extremely fortunate. He too was acquitted of all charges. Marion MacIngaroch was also brought to trial; her fate is not known.

There is little doubt that Katherine used witchcraft for her own ends. Her actions were not unusual among ladies of similar rank. Members of the noble classes frequently resorted to magic, whether for health, harm or love. Katherine's activities nearly cost her her life. It is almost certain that it was her position in society that saved her, whilst several less important people were condemned to burn.

The North Berwick Witches

The story of the North Berwick witch trials deserves to be singled out for special attention for a number of reasons. It was the first mass witch-trial to take place in Scotland and is notable for the numbers of people who were alleged, in the confessions of those who had been apprehended, to have been taking part in witchcraft in the area around East Lothian. The case also quickly achieved notoriety, even in those cruel times, for the manner in which some of those who were charged suffered for the accusations that had been made against them. The charges that were laid against the people accused of sorcery at North Berwick, and the confessions that were given by some of these people, not only demonstrate quite clearly how hard it is to distinguish the difference between fantasy and fact in cases of this nature, but also bring in an element that had not featured in previous witch trials in Scotland. This was the notion that the persons involved had been taking part in ceremonies and rites in which the Devil was said to have appeared; they had been consorting with and acting directly upon the wishes and demands of Satan himself.

Mention was made, for the first time in a Scottish witch trial, of the Satanic Pact, which swiftly became a major factor in establishing guilt in later prosecutions.

The North Berwick trials were also unique because of the personal part that King James VI played in the investigations and because the events that lead up to the trials involved two countries, Denmark and Scotland. Finally, but not least importantly, the trials of the North Berwick witches are particularly notable because the accused were charged not only with sorcery, but with treason, and the involvement of one of the accused, Francis Stewart, Earl of Bothwell, has been the subject of much debate amongst historians in the years that have passed since.

King James VI had chosen a wife for himself; the fourteen year-old Anne of Denmark. She was to be brought over to Scotland to marry him in 1589, but a succession of storms prevented the boat that was to bring her from setting sail. The Danish authorities blamed witchcraft for the unfortunate weather and consequently a number of people were arrested and brought to trial in Copenhagen. Eventually, King James agreed in the autumn of 1589 to travel overseas to Denmark to meet his betrothed and bring her back to Scotland himself. After a stay of some six months he returned with Anne, now his wife, to Scotland. His journey had been successfully accomplished, but it had been hampered by bad weather, both on the outward and return voyages. On the return voyage one of his ships, carrying wedding gifts for the new queen, was sunk.

In the closing weeks of 1690, the king received some disturbing news. It seemed that the evil that had hindered his marriage plans was not only to be found in Denmark. In his own land, witchcraft and treason were afoot. In North Berwick, a fishing port on the east coast of Scotland, a coven of witches had been working against the king, trying to cause his death through sorcery. The discovery had come to light in the following manner.

Suspicion had fallen first on a woman from Tranent, a servant of David Seton called Geillis Duncan, whose behaviour had caused her master some concern. The rather gruesome pamphlet *'Newes from Scotland'* published in 1591, described how the first suspicions were raised as follows:

'Within the towne of Trenent, in the kingdome of Scotland, there dwelleth one David Seaton who, being deputie bailiffe in the said towne, had a maid called Geillis Duncane, who used secretlie to absent and lie forth of hir maisters house every other night: This Geillis Duncan tooke in hand to helpe all such as were troubled or grieved with anie kinde of sicknes or infirmitie, and in short space did perfourme many matters most miraculous; which things, for asmuch as shee began to do them upon a sodaine, having never done the like before, made her maister and others to be in great admiration, and wondered thereat: by meanes whereof, the said David Seaton had his maid in great suspition that shee did not those things by naturall and lawfull waies, but rather supposed it to bee done by some extraordinarie and unlawfull meanes.'

So far, then, Geillis was not obviously guily of malefice. She kept disappearing at night, and she seemed to have a new and inexplicable ability to heal the sick. But if she could heal people, then she must also be capable of harm. On Seton's orders, Geillis was tortured – in all likelihood illegally – and examined for the Devil's mark, which was found on her neck. Following interrogation she confessed to having acted with others. More people were apprehended for investigation and over a relatively short space of time, a large number of names were produced, including the following: Agnes Sampson from Haddington, Agnes Thompson from Edinburgh, Doctor Fian from Prestonpans; the wife of George Motts from Lothian; Robert Grierson; Janet Sandilands, a potter's wife, a smith, Euphame Macalyean, Barbara Napier and several others from Edinburgh and East Lothian.

Agnes Sampson was the oldest and she was brought before King James himself for examination. She refused to give in to questioning and accordingly His Majesty ordered that she be taken to prison to be examined for the telltale mark of a witch and tortured until she confessed. The Devil's mark was found, and after suffering terrible tortures at the hands of her interrogators, Agnes admitted that she was a witch. She was brought in front of the king once more, and this time willingly told him about the treacherous and devilish deeds of which she and her accomplices were guilty. On Hallowe'en, 1589, she and several others had sailed in sieves, drinking and carousing all the way, to North Berwick. Dr Fian had taken the lead in the procession, with Geillis Duncan playing her jew's harp as musical accompaniment. The assembly of witches had danced their way towards the kirk, singing together:

> *Commer goe ye before, commer goe ye,*
> *Gif ye will not goe before, commer let me.*

This story was to be confirmed by Geillis Duncan, who was brought before King James to play her instrument for him to hear.

At the gathering in North Berwick, none other than Satan himself had been present, appearing in the shape of a man dressed in black. He had ordered that the king should be killed, and in a strange ceremony which had entailed the removal of joints from bodies buried within and without the kirkyard, the assembled persons had agreed to his wishes, sealing their promise by kissing the Devil's buttocks.

The king initially had strong misgivings about the reliability of Agnes Sampson's confession. He called her a liar. But Agnes, apparently, having previously refused so vehemently to give up a confession, was now quite eager to prove her guilt. She whispered in King James' ear the words that he had exchanged with his wife on their wedding night. Now would he believe that she was a witch? Of course he would.

The meeting at North Berwick might have been the largest meeting – accounts vary, but somewhere between forty and two hundred people were said to have attended – but it had not been the only one, according to the growing testimonies of various of the accused. At one other meeting, Dr Fian, Robert Grierson, Agnes Sampson and others had gone out to sea and had thrown a cat, delivered by the hand of Satan, into the water to try to prevent the king's ship from arriving safely back in Scotland. At another, with the Devil present, a stolen picture of the king was passed from hand to hand and trouble wished upon him. At another meeting, a wax likeness of King James VI was produced to assist the witches in the harm they intended. And on yet another occasion, venom from a toad which had been hung upside-down was mixed with urine and 'the thing in the forehead of a new-foaled foal' in an oyster-shell, ready to be left where it might fall upon the king and bring about his destruction.

Agnes Sampson, who had a reputation as a practising witch before the trial, was acknowledged in both age and status as the most senior of the women who were accused. She calmly gave long and detailed accounts of the witches' treasonable and maleficent activities, but her compliance did not bring her any benefits. She was strangled and burnt.

Dr Fian, the Prestonpans schoolmaster, proved to be equally forthcoming under torture and interrogation. He was generally acknowledged as the Devil's clerk in the proceedings at North Berwick – no doubt because he was one of the most educated among the gathering. He gave further information about the meeting at North Berwick kirk. It transpired he had a reputation as a womaniser and as a sorcerer and evidence was offered up by others against him to this effect.

Shortly after his confession had been secured, Fian escaped. He was caught again and in spite of his protests that his confession had been false, after further torture he faced the same fate as several of his co-accused.

Barbara Napier was a well-connected woman. Her husband, Archibald Douglas, was a respected citizen of Edinburgh. Her brother-in-law was an advocate. She admitted a connection with Richard Graham, one of the other accused, confessing that she had used his services as a magician on one occasion. She also admitted that she had had similar contact with Agnes Sampson. But throughout the entire proceeding, she denied taking part in any of the treasonable activities of which she had been accused. She had consulted witches, she said; but she was not guilty of practising witchcraft herself. She was initially cleared of the charge of treason, but following the intervention of the king, she was finally found guilty and executed.

Like Barbara Napier, Euphame Macalyean was a member of the Edinburgh gentry; the illegitimate daughter of one advocate, the wife of another. The accusations against her not only involved her alleged participation in the activities of the North Berwick witches, but also her alleged conspiracy to kill her first husband with witchcraft and her use of witchcraft in matters of love and personal dispute. In spite of a powerful legal defence, Euphame Macalyean was found guilty and burned alive.

Richard Graham, another of the accused, also had a reputation as a sorcerer. He was already an excommunicate. He was acknowledged as one of the most powerful figures in the group and may even have been the leader. It was he who commanded Geillis Duncan to assemble with the other witches at North Berwick. He was acquainted with several members of the Scottish nobility who were said to have recognised and at times made use of his magical powers. He confessed to having 'raised the Devil' on more than one occasion. Graham survived longer than most of the other accused, but he, too was eventually executed in 1592.

The confessions of Agnes Sampson, Geillis Duncan, Richard Graham and others all named Francis Stewart, the Earl of Bothwell as the man behind their attempts to kill the king. Bothwell was a powerful figure in Scotland, and had been one of the members of the Regency Council in charge of Scottish affairs while James was away in Denmark, but his relationship with the king was not a comfortable one and it was believed by many that he did indeed pose a threat to the king's security. Whether he had been the figure behind all the intrigue, or whether the allegations of his involvement in the affair were prompted, or manufactured by his political enemies will never be known. He did acknowledge that Richard Graham was known to him, but strenuously denied any part in a magical conspiracy against the king. And whilst proceedings against the other accused moved quite swiftly to a conclusion (although Richard Graham was not executed until 1592, most of those who had been found guilty had been executed by spring 1591), Bothwell's case was to occupy the king's mind for considerably longer. Richard Graham had told in his confession of several meetings which had taken place at which he and Bothwell had discussed how best the king's death might be caused by enchantment. During his period of imprisonment, he also claimed that Bothwell had sent him money in an attempt to bribe him into keeping silent about any such activities.

Bothwell was eventually arrested in May 1591 and imprisoned in Edinburgh Castle. He had several points to bring up in his own defence: Graham was an unreliable witness, as were the other witches who had named him; Graham had been persuaded to make the allegations against him with promises of avoiding execution. But by June, James had been convinced that Bothwell was guilty of treasonable conspiracy, and plans were made to send him into exile abroad. Bothwell foiled the king's plans to send him out of harm's way, however, for he managed to escape and went north into hiding. The king had him declared a traitor and his goods were forfeited to the crown, but Bothwell remained at liberty for two more years, tormenting King James in mind and, on one occasion, threatening him in person at Holyrood Palace. Finally, in 1593, he was brought to trial. King James was not to see Bothwell brought to justice on this occasion either, however, for Bothwell maintained his innocence. His case rested principally on Graham's proven reputation as a sorcerer and hence his unreliability as a witness, and on the claim that Graham had been coerced into manufacturing evidence against him. Bothwell was not short of powerful supporters and few people were surprised when he was acquitted of the charges against him.

It is quite likely that there was a conspiracy to kill King James in 1589–90, and that those who took part in it sought to achieve their ends through the use of black magic. Just how much of the confessions of Agnes Sampson, John Fian, Geillis Duncan and others can be taken as fact will never be known. If everything that was laid against those that were accused is to believed, then the conspiracy was certainly far-reaching. From Edinburgh, to Prestonpans, to North Berwick, there were groups of people from all walks of life who had some part in the affair. Just how many people really were involved will also remain a mystery, for although we know the fates of the more notable figures in the case, we do not know how many others were apprehended and tried for their alleged role in the sorry business.

The role of the Devil in the witches' activities continues to invite speculation. Was this one individual coordinating all efforts, appearing to the witches in demonic guise? Might it have been different men (for the Devil appeared in the form of a man) on different occasions – Richard Graham on one occasion, someone else on others. Or might it even have been Bothwell himself? Did Bothwell instigate the whole affair, or were the allegations of his involvement the result of his enemies, or more specifically, supporters of the king, conspiring to put him out of harm's way? Did Agnes Sampson, Richard Graham and the others who named Bothwell, willingly volunteer Bothwell's name or was it suggested to them? Bothwell was known as a loose cannon, to say the least, and had already been involved in rebellion against the king before 1589. He did know Richard Graham, and had even made use of Graham's skills as a sorcerer in the past. Might he have called upon Graham to help him to get rid of the king and throw the country into chaos? If so, why? Historians are likely to be intrigued by the case for years to come.

Margaret Barclay of Irvine

Margaret Barclay was married to Archibald Dean, a respectable citizen of Irvine, Renfrewshire and a burgess of the town. Her husband had a brother called John Dean, who was married to a woman called Janet. Margaret, it would appear, had a fiery temper. One day in 1618, a quarrel arose between Margaret and her brother- and sister-in-law over the alleged theft of some money, during which Janet called Margaret a thief and Margaret allegedly cursed Janet. The dispute simmered on until eventually Margaret was moved to take the matter to the kirk session, accusing Janet of slander. The members of the kirk session (quite rightly) did not treat the affair very seriously, and ordered the two women to bury their differences. This they agreed to do, and it seemed as if the whole matter was over. Then Margaret was heard to say that she had only agreed to renew her friendship with her sister-in-law to keep in favour with the kirk session. In her opinion, the dispute was far from over and she held John and Janet in as much contempt as ever.

John Dean was the captain of a merchant ship, owned by the provost of Irvine, Andrew Train. When John's ship next set sail from Irvine laden with cargo for foreign parts, Margaret was heard to utter a curse as she watched it sailing out of harbour. Whether her feelings towards her brother-in-law were as murderous as the words of her curse implied, she would soon regret that she had been overheard.

Time passed and no news was heard of the ship until one day, the provost's wife received a visit from a stranger, a travelling performer called John Stewart. John informed the good lady that the merchant ship had been lost at sea, with her husband on board. Shortly afterwards, the official news reached the town that the ship had indeed been lost; it had sunk with all hands off the south coast of England. Now Margaret Barclay's curse came back to haunt her.

Rumours turned into accusations and Margaret Barclay was arrested on suspicion of witchcraft. John Stewart was also arrested on account of his apparent ability to foretell the future.

John Stewart's first reaction was to try to clear his own name by implicating Margaret in attempted sorcery. He told his interrogators that she had approached him with a request for initiation into the magical arts – taking cows' milk, finding love, getting revenge, taking food, etc. Of course, he told his audience, he could not help her, for he had no knowledge of things like that. He was not believed. He was instead subjected to more strenuous investigations, under torture, and this time his interrogators were rewarded with a much more satisfying story. He told them he had gone to Margaret Barclay's house and found her and two other women, whom he later identified as Isobel Insh and Isobel Crawford, busily engaged in constructing figures of people from clay. These were supposed to represent Provost Train, John Dean, and members of the ship's crew. Isobel Insh's young daughter had also been there, according to Stewart. The women had also made a clay model of a ship, presumably the provost's ship. As the women worked away, Stewart said that he had seen a black dog appear, which he presumed was the Devil. The women and the dog had then taken the figures down to the seashore and had thrown them into the water. The waves had turned wild, and the roaring waters had turned red 'like the juice of a madder in a dyer's cauldron'.

Isobel Insh and her daughter – who was only eight years old – were brought before the kirk session for questioning. The little girl, probably terrified by the whole experience, admitted to having been present when the women made the clay models of the people and the ship. She also agreed that a black dog had been there, adding that flames had come from its nose and mouth, and she said that a black man had helped the women to make the figures. Isobel Insh, at first strenuously denying any involvement in the affair, eventually gave in under pressure of questioning (and possibly physical persuasion). She admitted her presence in the house when the figures were being made, and confessed to having supernatural powers.

Isobel Insh was detained in the church steeple to await further questioning. That night, driven mad with terror, she tried to escape by climbing out of a window in the roof. She fell several feet to the ground and sustained injuries from which she died a few days later.

Stewart's attempts to secure his own liberty by delating others were in vain. He was put under torture on the orders of the Earl of Eglinton. He stuck to his story regarding Margaret Barclay and the three other women and admitted his supernatural gift of telling the future, saying he had been given it after meeting the King of Fairies in Ireland some years previously. He was locked up pending his trial, but chose to avoid the ordeal ahead by taking his own life. He hanged himself from the doorhandle of his cell with a string which he had taken from his bonnet, and although he was not quite dead when they first found him, he died very soon after.

Margaret Barclay and Isobel Crawford remained of the four. Margaret Barclay was the first of the two to point the finger of accusation. Until this point, she had maintained her innocence vehemently. There was very little evidence to point to her guilt, except a sprig of rowan and a length of red thread – a known charm *against* witches – that had been found in her possession, and the testament of John Stewart, himself a confessed witch. But the Earl of Eglinton had recommended 'gentle' torture be applied to the two women, and in Margaret Barclay's case we know that this consisted of placing iron bars upon her outstretched legs one at a time until the weight and pain grew unbearable. Eventually a confession was forced out of her and she named Isobel Crawford. Isobel Crawford, in her turn, also gave in, confessed to having taken part in the clay figure making, and blamed Margaret Barclay as the instigator of the sorry affair.

Almost as soon as Margaret's pains were at an end, she retracted her confession, stating, quite correctly, that it had been obtained under torture. But in spite of this, and a last-minute appearance by her husband to plead on her behalf, her hopes of mercy were in vain. She was found guilty as charged. When she retracted her confession, Margaret also stated quite categorically that she had falsely accused Isobel Crawford, but the court remained unmoved by her pleas, and delivered another guilty verdict. Both women were sentenced to death.

It is unlikely that Margaret Barclay was guilty of more than bad temper and the the inability to let an argument rest. Her temper, the inopportune arrival of John Stewart – who was undoubtedly little more than a scandalmonger and a liar – and the superstitious beliefs of the church authorities had combined to cause her own death, and that of three other people.

Alexander Hamilton, Elizabeth Steven and Katharine Oswald of East Lothian

Alexander Hamilton, a warlock by repute, was taken captive in 1629 and imprisoned in the tolbooth in Edinburgh. Under questioning, Alexander delated several other persons for being guilty of witchcraft. Nine women from the area in and around Haddington were apprehended as a result of Hamilton's accusations, and the Privy Council ordered for them to be detained and investigated in Haddington.

The fate of the nine Haddington women is not known, but another woman whom Hamilton accused, Katharine Oswald from Niddry, was to suffer terribly for the accusations. Katharine Oswald had also been delated by another woman Elizabeth Steven, who had recently been executed for witchcraft herself. Elizabeth's accusations had been maintained from her imprisonment right until the moment she faced death at the stake. In spite of the protestations of Katharine's defence that the word of a confessed witch, who might be deluded, and the word of an accused warlock, who was a notorious liar, should not be taken as genuine witness statements, the court accepted Elizabeth Steven's pre-execution statement and Alexander Hamilton's statement under oath as being true. Alexander Hamilton maintained that he had been present at several witch meetings with Katharine Oswald, between Niddry and Edmonstone, and at Prestonpans. They had met with the Devil, according to Hamilton, and at one of the meetings, in the presence of the Devil, Katharine Oswald had had sexual intercourse with Hamilton. A number of other charges were laid against Katharine Oswald. As in so many other cases of witchcraft, once one accusation had been made, several others followed. It was claimed that she had practised witchcraft both for the purpose of curing and for causing harm. Amongst those whom she was said to have cured with magic was a man named John Niddery, who had been suffering from the 'trembling fever'. One of her alleged malefices involved giving a cow mastitis. Katharine had offered to buy the cow in question from a man called John Nisbet, but he had turned her down. The cow had then given blood instead of milk for some days after that – a clear sign, it was alleged, of Katharine's evil at work.

All the protests of Katharine Oswald's defence were rejected. She was found guilty as charged and was executed in 1629.

Alexander Hamilton, having helped to seal the fate of at least one other and perhaps several more, now faced judgement himself. He had admitted his presence at witch-meetings; this had been the substance of his accusations against Katharine Oswald. At his own trial the following year, it was revealed that Hamilton had encountered the Devil for the first time in East Lothian. Having undertaken to become the Devil's servant, Hamilton was instructed that he could summon his master by striking the ground three times with a stick, and shouting, 'Rise up, foul thief!' He had met with the Devil since then, not only at witch-meetings, but also on his own. The Devil appeared to him in different shapes; sometimes a dog, at other times as a cat or a crow. Hamilton was found guilty of various malefices, including the burning of a mill full of corn by magic. In addition to his admissions of renouncing his baptism, following the Devil and practising witchcraft, of course there was also his admission of sexual misconduct with Katharine Oswald; a transgression which was taken seriously by the authorities, in particular by the Kirk in those days. He would be viewed as all the more wicked for this.

Alexander Hamilton was executed in January 1630.

Another person whom Alexander Hamilton had accused was Lady Home of Manderston. She was guilty, he claimed, of having tried to kill her husband, Sir George Home, through witchcraft. The evidence against her was slight, and Sir George was unavailable to appear as a witness (he was avoiding the legal authorities on account of his own debt problems). Accordingly, the case went nowhere. Then in 1631, another case came to light in which Sir George Home's name appeared. Apparently, he had been the intended victim of malefice at the hands of another. Whether this connects with the accusations which Alexander Hamilton made against Sir George's wife can only be a matter of conjecture, but the possibility must not be overlooked. A man called John Neill from Tweedmouth was brought to trial on charges of witchcraft. Some of the charges against him related to healing. On one particular occasion he had, it was said, cured a man's illness by instructing the man's wife to wash his shirt in south-running water and then put it back on him. But the other charges concerned Neill's alleged meetings with the Devil and attempts to harm Sir George Home by witchcraft. Neill had convened with a group of witches on Coldingham Law (in Berwickshire) and this was where the plans to destroy Sir George had been made. The magic consisted of:

> *'Getting ane enchanted dead foal, and putting it in Sir George's stable, under his horse's manger, and putting a dead hand enchanted by the Devil in Sir George's garden in Berwick; by which enchantments Sir George contracted a grievous disease, of which he could not be recovered till the said foal and hand were discovered and burnt.'*

Was John Neill (who was accused along with two women, Katherine Wilson and Alie Nisbet) in league with Alexander Hamilton, or with Lady Home? In all likelihood he was in league with Alexander Hamilton, for his two co-accused had been among those who were delated by Hamilton before he was executed. It was acknowledged that there was considerable and long-standing enmity between Lady Home and her husband, and it may be that, wishing to dispose of him, she sought the services of known witches. She certainly would not be the first member of the Scottish gentry to resort to such measures.

As with so many cases, the truth will never be known. John Neill and Alie Nisbet were both executed for witchcraft. Katharine Wilson was eventually acquitted after successfully claiming that evidence had been manufactured against her, but her reputation would probaly remain with her long after, in spite of her acquittal.

Agnes Finnie of Edinburgh

The name of Agnes Finnie may already be familiar to some of those who have taken part in 'witch' tours around Scotland's capital city, which in recent years have made her as famous in Edinburgh's Old Town as she was when she was alive.

Agnes Finnie was a trader in Edinburgh, a fishwife from

Potterrow with a sharp tongue and a foul temper; spiteful in the extreme, but also a victim of the terrible spite of others. She was tried for witchcraft in 1642, and there was no shortage of people to come forward and testify to her malevolence and the damage that she allegedly caused. She was clearly a woman who had made more than her fair share of enemies. The blame for deaths, sicknesses and a variety of other misfortunes was piled upon poor Agnes Finnie and her fate was inevitable from the outset.

Agnes may not have been fair in her financial dealings with other people, for several of the complaints against her stemmed from arguments about money. A woman called Beatrice Nisbet borrowed some money from Agnes and an argument was started over the terms of the loan. Agnes became very angry when Beatrice refused to repay the money owed with interest, and shortly after they had quarrelled, Beatrice lost the power of speech. An argument between Agnes and Bessie Currie over money ended badly for Bessie; Agnes cursed Bessie, saying the Devil would bite her, and caused Bessie's husband, John Buchanan to become sick with a terrible illness. A third argument over money began when Agnes refused a woman called Janet Grinton a refund for some fish that she had sold her that were bad. Agnes cursed Janet, and not long after the altercation, Janet became unable to eat and subsequently died. A fourth argument arose when Agnes fell out with a woman called Christian Dickson over a loan. Agnes resolved the argument, as usual, with a curse.

Agnes was not wholly malevolent in her dealings with other people. When the child of John Buchanan and Bessie Currie fell ill, Agnes visited it and made an attempt at effecting a cure. But her efforts were in vain, and the child died. Once again, Agnes's name was linked with disaster.

As argument followed argument and customers and neighbours fell prey to more misfortunes, rumours were spreading about

Agnes Finnie. One of the things to which Agnes took particular exception, apparently, was name-calling. One cheeky lad who had insulted her found himself paralysed down one side after she lost her temper with him. Sometimes, she was called a witch to her face; in those days, of course, this was much more than mere name-calling. To call someone a witch was to attach a label to them which attracted real danger, and Agnes was understandably distressed. The manner in which she dealt with the accusations, however, only made things worse. When Euphame Kincaid called her a witch, Agnes retaliated with a curse. Shortly afterwards, Euphame's daughter's leg was broken in an accident. Like mother, like daughter, it seems, for Agnes's daughter Margaret was also said to have reacted badly when someone called her a witch's child. The name-caller was suitably punished when her husband lost his mind.

Over time, with the help of unfortunate coincidence, Agnes Finnie managed to dig a hole for herself so deep that she could not hope to get out. Finally, inevitably, she was brought to trial, to face an overwhelming body of evidence. We do not know whether Agnes had any friends, but it is clear that her enemies were numerous, and had been eager to add their twopence worth to the pile. She was found guilty of witchcraft and executed on Castle Hill.

Robert 'Hob' Grieve

The story of Hob Grieve is told in 'Satan's Invisible World Discovered', written by George Sinclair and published in 1685.

Hob Grieve was a man from Lauder, who was taken into custody in 1649, accused of being a warlock. In spite of persistent questioning, Grieve strenuously denied all the charges that were laid against him and held out against his interrogators for a considerable period of time. At length, however, the persistence of his captors was rewarded and Hob eventually confessed that he was guilty. He had accepted the Devil as his master and had worked in his service for approximately eighteen years.

It was known that Hob's wife had been a witch; she had been charged with witchcraft and burned at the stake several years ago. Grieve told his interrogators that it was she who had persuaded him to renounce his baptism and enter the service of the Devil. The couple had been very poor at the time, and Hob's wife had offered her husband an escape from poverty. In fact, she had tempted him with the promise of becoming rich in the Devil's service.

In order that her husband might finally be persuaded, Hob's wife had taken him to meet the Devil one night by Gallow Water. At first, all had been quiet, but after they had waited for a long time, they suddenly saw a large black dog running past in the darkness. Hob was panicked by this, but his wife reassured him and shortly afterwards, the Devil appeared before them in the shape of a man. The Devil was full of promises: he would make Hob rich, he would give him great standing in the community. At length, Hob was won over. He agreed to enter Satan's service.

In his confession, Hob stressed that it was not the promise of wealth that persuaded him, but instead it was the fear of what might happen to him if he refused the Devil. The Devil had given him the duty of summoning the witches to their meetings, and he had performed this service faithfully until he was apprehended by the authorities.

Hob's confession was quite detailed. Not only did he confess to his own wrongdoing; he also delated several other witches, all of whom eventually confessed after interrogation. One woman, however, had been more than a little reluctant to surrender her confession. She had been warned before her arrest – it was said the warning came from the Devil himself – that Hob had delated her for witchcraft. Enraged, she came to the tolbooth where Hob was imprisoned, and demanded the chance to confront him. When she was finally taken to meet him, the outcome of their meeting was not what she had intended. Far from retracting his accusation, Hob reminded the woman of all that she had done, and persuaded her to confess in front of witnesses.

Following their confessions, and before sentence was carried out, Hob and the other witches were taken to church and there, we are told, it seemed that they were compelled to see the error of putting their trust in the Devil. They were astounded to realise at last that the Devil had lured them into his service with trickery and rather than wishing good for his servants, sought nothing but the destruction of their souls. Hob Grieve stood up in church and bore witness to this fact. He told the rest of the congregation how he had nearly drowned on one occasion in the river at Musselburgh and this, he knew, was the Devil's work. Having thus confessed his sins and acknowledged his terrible mistakes with such evangelical zeal, Hob and his fellow witches were lead away to face their fate.

The witches were all executed for their pains; but they went to their deaths, according to Sinclair, having renounced Satan and asked the forgiveness of God.

There is a tragic adjunct to this terrible tale, for Sinclair goes on to tell us of the fate of another woman, who was imprisoned at the same time, having been delated by some other person as a witch. She had not confessed to the charges against her. When she learned that the other witches were about to be burned, she fell into terrible despair. She had not been sentenced to death, but still had little hope of being set free. Even if she might eventually secure her freedom, she knew only too well that her reputation would be such that her life would not be worth living in the community to which she had belonged. The prospect of rotting alone in prison terrified her. The prospect of potential release was not much better. Death seemed like the only means of escape from her predicament. The woman summoned the ministers and magistrates and told them that when she had been a young girl she had met with the Devil and entered his service. He had kissed her and given her a new name. She was suspected of having manufactured the confession in order to end her life. Indeed, it was believed that the Devil was tempting her to do so. But she persisted with her story under questioning from both ministers and magistrates and finally she was tried, found guilty and sentenced to die in the same manner as the other witches. Her execution must have been a desperately pitiful occasion, for as she was about to die, she told the assembled crowd what she had done. She admitted that she had made her confession in order to end her own life. Accused but not guilty of one crime, that of witchcraft, she had been so tormented that she had confessed, and had thus committed another terrible offence against God. For what she had done was virtually suicide. She had caused her own premature death by making execution inevitable.

Marie Lamont of Inverkip

Marie Lamont was only eighteen years old when she was charged with witchcraft in 1662. Her account of her crimes, offered voluntarily if the records are to be believed (she claimed to have been urged by God to confess), is remarkable for having in it so many elements that concur exactly with many of the widely-held beliefs that were held at that time about witches, their powers and the manner of things of which they were capable.

Marie said that she had been a witch for some five years, having been converted by another local woman, named Kathrein, or Katie, Scot. Katie had shown Marie how to steal milk from her neighbour's cow by magic. Marie told of her first meeting with the Devil and of her conversion. When asked to give herself up to his service, it seems that she did so willingly. She described a fairly typical scenario; placing one hand on the crown of her head, another on the sole of her foot, and giving all between the two to the Devil. In common with many other confessing witches, Marie claimed to have been given a different name by Satan. She was called 'Clowts'. She was to address the Devil as 'Serpent'. The Devil marked her on her right side, by nipping her.

Marie named at least four accomplices in her confession, and it transpired that their malefices as a group involved much more than the mere taking of milk. One of their evil deeds was an act of revenge. One of the women in the group, Margaret Holm, had been evicted from her house by a man called Allan Orr. In response to this harsh treatment, Margaret had placed a curse on Orr. She and her fellow witches, transformed into the shape of cats, had gone to Orr's home and had taken a bite from one of the fish in the herring barrel that was stored there. When Orr and his wife had shortly afterwards made a meal of the affected fish, they had fallen ill and rapidly died.

Marie and her accomplices had met the Devil in the guise of a brown dog one night. Together they had planned to raise storms and cause havoc for the fishermen in the area. Once, they had caused a wind strong enough to tear the sails from a ship belonging to a man called Colin Campbell.

The minister, being a particular enemy of the Devil's, had also fallen prey to the evil attentions of the witches. The Devil had met them again, this time in the guise of a black man with cloven feet, and directed operations, turning them into cats to carry out their duties.

Milk stealing, shape-changing, weather-changing, the sinking of ships, the causing of sickness and death – each of these activities were common elements in witch belief and tales of witch activities. It must have gladdened the hearts of the Kirk Session members to know that they had in their grasp one woman who confessed to all of the above. Not only that, but the information supplied about the Devil and Marie's other accomplices confirmed many current beliefs about practitioners of the Black Arts. Satan appeared to them in different guises – a brown dog, a cloven-footed black man. His followers acted according to a specific hierarchy. According to Marie:

'in that business some were chiefs and ringleaders, others were but followers'.

The meetings of the witches had many of the hallmarks of Satanic rituals – drinking, bawdy merriment and dancing. Marie's account of the witches' conversion by the Devil was also fairly typical. After persuading the women to renounce their baptism, Satan marked his followers as his own to seal the Demonic Pact (Marie was marked with a nip), and gave them new names. When he left them, he kissed them.

There are certain things about this case that might give us cause to doubt whether Marie Lamont was really a witch as she claimed. Firstly, the fact that she felt moved to confess in the first place is most unusual. She would be aware of the likely fate that awaited her following her confession. Why would she voluntarily submit to such a fate when most other witches had to have such information dragged out of them?

Secondly, her story conforms to so many standard witch beliefs held in Scotland at the time. She accused herself of several different kinds of malefice of witches were believed capable, and yet there is no mention of any complaint having been made against her, in spite of the fact that her behaviour, if she did all these

115

things ought to have aroused suspicions in the community. We have to wonder whether Marie was acting out some sort of fantasy, concocting a story about herself gleaned from all she had learned about the mysteries of witchcraft.

It would have been enough if Marie had confessed to renouncing her baptism, receiving the Devil's mark and carrying out just one act of malefice. That would have secured her conviction. But her story contained so much more. It was a gift to her accusers, and a blow struck against all those who might dare to express any scepticism regarding the dangers of witchcraft or reluctance to pursue those who were guilty. Marie's fate is not recorded, but after such a confession, she is unlikely to have escaped with her life.

Isobel Gowdie

Mention has already been made several times of the confessions of Isobel Gowdie of Auldearn. The case of Isobel Gowdie stands out from all the records of prosecutions for witchcraft in Scotland because of the richness of the confessions that she offered up after being apprehended. Isobel Gowdie, the wife of John Gilbert of Lochloy, was delated as a witch in 1662 along with another woman called Janet Braidhead. We do not know what were the events leading up to Isobel's confession, in the kirk at Auldearn, but according to the transcription, no undue force was used to persuade her to speak. Whatever it was that prompted her to admit her crimes, it appears that once her defences were down, her secrets spilled out unabated. Over a period of six weeks or so, Isobel made four separate confessions in total, which contained all the elements of current beliefs about witch practices in Scotland, and more. If anything was believed possible of a witch, then Isobel claimed she had done it. In the many years that have followed, all those who have read of Isobel

Gowdie, whether historians or simply people with a lively interest in Scottish history, have wondered what was the truth that lay behind the stories related by this woman to her audience in the kirk at Auldearn. Most people are willing to accept that Gowdie did believe herself to be a practising witch, and that there were others who shared her beliefs and with her, took part in activities that were intentionally maleficient. It also seems clear that whether or not any of the group's activities did in fact result in harm to their intended victims, or were merely coincidental with misfortunes that befell these people, Gowdie and her fellow witches believed that their magic was effective. Much of what she said was confirmed by the confession of Janet Braidhead, and although there is no record of the ultimate fate of the two women, we must have little doubt that they were strangled and burned, as would be only fit in the eyes of their prosectutors.

Gowdie's account of renouncing her baptism and giving herself into the service of Satan would confirm all the beliefs of her prosecutors about such matters. It contained all the necessary elements. It was straightforward and to the point:

'As I was going betwixt the towns of Drumdewin and the Heads, I met with the Devill, and there covenanted in a manner with him. And I promised to meet him in the night time in the Kirk of Auldearn, whilk I did. And the first thing I did there that night, I denyed my baptism, and did put the one of my hands to the crowne of my head, and the other to the sole of my foot, and then renuncit all betwixt my two hands, to the Devill."'

Janet Braidhead's account of her own conversion was very similar, but she stated that her introduction to the Devil had come through her husband, John Taylor. She then went on to describe her marking and baptism by the Devil:

'. . . .*my husband presented me, and he and Margaret Wilson in Auldearn, held me up to the Divell to be baptised. . . .the Divell marked me in the shoulder, and suked out my blood with his mouth at that place; he spowted it in his hand, and sprinkled it on my head.*'

Isobel Gowdie's first confession told in detail of several meetings with the Devil and other witches, and described a number of their activities. These included having carnal knowledge of the Devil, changing straws into horses, meeting with the Queen of the Fairies, stealing milk from cattle by magic, stealing the strength from other people's ale by magic, meddling with Alexander Cumming's dyeworks so that only black dye was produced, and, worst of all, conspiring to destroy the Laird of Park's children, using image magic. Gowdie named more than fifteen other people who were involved in her evil deeds with her, described the Devil's changing appearance, and talked about the coven of which she was a member, which numbered thirteen witches, and other covens with which her own was associated.

Her second confession repeated many elements of the first and gave more information. She told her audience that the witches were given nicknames, and all had attendant spirits:

'*I remember not all the Spiritis names: bot thair is one called "Swein" whilk waitis upon the said Margret Wilson in Auldearn; he is still* (always) *clothed in grass-green; and the said Margret Wilson has an niknam called "Pikle neirest the Wind".*'

The commander of the spirits, according to Isobel, was called 'Robert the Rule'. (This name is quite similar to 'Robert the Rower, or Robert the Comptroller', the nickname which Robert Grierson, one of the North Berwick witches, was said to have had.)

Isobel told her audience how the witches used magic to raise the wind, how elf-arrows were made by the Devil and his 'Elf boys', and how the witches used the arrows:

'We have no bow to shoot with, but sprang them from the naillis of our thumbes. Some tymes we will misse, bot if they twitch (touch), *be it beast, or man or woman, it will kill. . . .'*

There was a charm for every occasion, and in the course of her confessions Isobel Gowdie took the time to recite several to her listeners: charms for changing the witches into hares, cats, or crows – and back again, charms for curing fever, sores and sciatica, charms for taking fish, spoiling crops and stealing crops and charms for making people sick, sicker, or dead. In particular, Gowdie gave a detailed description the witches' efforts to make Harry Forbes, minister of the parish of Auldearn suffer. Harry Forbes was already unwell, and the witches wanted to prolong his illness. Having made a 'bag' against him (a concoction of gall's flesh, toads' guts, barley, finger and toenail clippings, a hare's liver and bits of cloth), they soaked it in water and recited the following rhyme:

'He is lying in his bed – and he is seik and sair,
Let him lie intil that bed two months and three days mair;
Let him lie intil his bed – let him lie intil it seik and sair,
Let him lie intil his bed months two and three days mair;
He shall lie intil his bed – he shall lie in it seik and sair,
He shall lie intil his bed two months and three days mair.'

One slightly comic element crept into Isobel Gowdie's second confession. She let her audience in on the secret of slipping away from the marital bed unnoticed:

'And least our husbands should miss us owt of our beddis, we put in a boosom (a broom), *or a thrie leggit stool besyde them, and then say thrice ower:*

"I lay down this boosom (or stool) in the Devillis name,
Let it not stir. . . . .While I come again."

'And immediatlie it seimis a woman beside owr husbandis.'

It is most likely that Isobel Gowdie's confession was gathered from a list of responses to questions asked by her prosecutors. As we do not know what the questions were, we cannot determine how much prompting she needed to give such a rich amount of detail, or how leading were the questions asked of her. But by the time the reader gets to the third confession, he or she must wonder whether Isobel Gowdie was in any way making the most of her opportunity to shock. Her fate, we can reasonably assume, had been sealed, for she had admitted that she was a witch. Was she driven to elaborate her story to this extent by her interrogators, or was she acting out of defiance – or madness?

Perhaps Isobel's surname – Gowdie, meaning 'goldy' – indicates that she came from a family of redheads, but this may not have been the case. Her third confession gives us a better idea of her age and appearance. She was clearly not an old woman, and in all likelihood quite attractive, and was at pains to indicate this fact, as she gave further details of her relationship with the Devil. Whether she was goaded on by lewd curiosity on the part of her interrogators, or was boldly brazen in the face of adversity, it seems certain that Isobel displayed a certain amount of personal pride in her descriptions of the physical relations that she and some of the others had with the Devil. She told how Jean Martin, the 'maiden' in the coven, sat next to the Devil, with Isobel and other younger women close by:

'. . . .*all the old people. . . .he cairis not for, and are weak and unmeet for him.*'

Sexual intercourse between Isobel and the Devil was frequent and fulfilling, apparently, and she gave descriptions of both his physical attributes and his sexual prowess. With herself and some of the other witches, the Devil was, she said,

'*lyk a weath-horse after mearis* (mares),'

and

'*He would lye with us in preference of all the multitude.*'

In spite of this, the Devil could be a cruel master. Sometimes he beat the witches cruelly, said Gowdie:

'*We would be beattin if we were absent any tyme, or neglect any thing that would be appointit to be done.*'

Was it with a note of scorn that she told of one particular man's reaction to this treatment?

'*Alex Elder, in Earlfeat, would be verie oft beattin. He is but soft, and could never defend him self in the least, but greitt and cry, when he would be scourging him.*'

Isobel also gave, with admitted regret, a list of the people whom she had killed (or believed she had killed) with elf-arrows. She

121

repeated her account of the conspiracy to destroy the Laird of Park's children using a clay image, and described how the witches had stolen and feasted upon an ox. Her fourth confession reiterated much of what had been said before.

Isobel Gowdie and Janet Braidhead incriminated more than thirty other people in their confessions, prompting further arrests. As events following Isobel Gowdie's confession are unknown, we can only guess at the havoc that was created in the district after she had told her terrible secrets to the kirk session, but if Isobel Gowdie sought notoriety, she certainly achieved it, for no account of witchcraft in Scotland is complete without the story of her confessions.

Major Thomas Weir and Grizel Weir

The case of Major Thomas Weir is very different from the vast majority of cases of witchcraft recorded in Scotland. While most of the witches who were tried and executed were brought to the attention of the Kirk Sessions and courts following accusations made by neighbours or relatives, and most of the confessions resulted from questioning and sometimes physical pressure, Major Weir's confession was entirely voluntary, unprompted and, given his reputation in the part of Edinburgh in which he lived, completely unexpected. At the time of his confession in 1670, Major Weir was living in a rented house in the West Bow, a street leading down to the Grassmarket in Edinburgh. He shared his house with his unmarried sister, Grizel. He was a retired soldier, fiercely anti-Catholic and anti-Royalist, and was described as a serious man, 'of grim countenance', always dressed in black. Wherever he went, he carried a black staff. A member of a strict Presbyterian sect, he seemed to live a particularly pious life and was held in high esteem by other members of his church. He held frequent prayer meetings in his own home, leading the prayers with a fervour that was quite inspirational. He appears to have been a figure who was held in considerable awe in the community. It was only after his own confession that stories about the strange behaviour of the good Major started to reach the ears of the authorities.

Weir's confession came quite out of the blue. He was attending a religious service when he suddenly stood up and started to accuse himself of being in the service of the Devil. The first reaction of the other members of the congregation was disbelief. The Major was quite clearly ill. Something had caused him to lose his senses; 'Angelic' Thomas, as he was known amongst them, was raving like a madman. Members of the church tried to reason with him, to calm him down, but Weir was implacable.

Weir persisted with his claims, and medical advice was sought. Doctors declared him to be mentally disturbed. The authorities were initially very reluctant to prosecute him. However, he remained absolutely insistent that he was guilty of terrible sins, for which he was not seeking any sort of pardon, and at length he was imprisoned in the tolbooth while further investigations were made. He had implicated his sister Grizel in his crimes, and she, too, was arrested. Much to the surprise of all concerned, Grizel corroborated her brother's stories. Major Weir's black staff was taken from him, for they claimed that he had been given it by none other than the Devil himself, and it was an instrument of terrible power.

Weir's confession detailed, amongst other things, an incestuous relationship with Grizel, and various other unnatural sexual practices. Grizel confirmed that what he said was true. Grizel, the quiet spinster sister, was transformed by her brother's and her own confession into Grizel the necromancer, with the ability to spin yarn at unnatural speed, yarn which would break the moment anyone tried to weave with it. Grizel proudly showed off a mark on her forehead, in the shape of a horseshoe, which appeared when she frowned. It was the mark given to her by the Devil, she said. She confessed that much of what she and Thomas knew had been learned from their mother, who had been a witch. She also told of a dark stranger taking herself and the Major to Dalkeith in a fiery coach.

There was no alternative but to take Major Weir and Grizel to trial – but rather than charge a former pillar of the church with witchcraft, (in spite of Weir's willing admission that he practised the black arts), the church authorities chose, in what may have been a face-saving exercise, to charge both brother and sister with unnatural sexual practices. Throughout his trial both Weir and his sister remained unrepentant. Guilty was the only verdict. Grizel was sentenced to hang. The Major was to be strangled and burnt. Both remained defiant until death. As the rope was tightened around his neck, the Major is said to have refused to ask for God's mercy. His staff was thrown into the flames beside its master. Both are said to have taken an exceptionally long time to burn, and witnesses claimed to have seen the staff twisting and jumping as the flames crackled around it. Grizel's hanging was no less dramatic. As preparations were made to end her life on the scaffold, she tried desperately to remove all her clothes in front of the assembled crowds in a last defiant affront to decency.

After the initial shock of the arrests and executions had died down, more stories began to spread about Thomas and Grizel's life. People who lived in the area of the West Bow where the brother and sister had lived said there had been some strange goings-on at their house. There were lights and noises in the building at odd hours of the night, the figure of a female, twice the height of a normal woman, appearing outside, laughing maniacally and terrifying passers-by, torch-bearing fiends shrieking and roaring in the streets nearby. The Major's staff was said to have been able to run errands for him, to answer the door, and to move down the street independently of its master as he walked from place to place.

Such was the notoriety of the case that Major Weir and his sister lived on in the imaginations of the people of Edinburgh for years to come. Their house (long since gone) became a place of fear, reputed to be haunted. It lay empty for many years before anyone could be persuaded to live in it again. Strange sights, fearful sounds and malevolent presences were reported in the area. It is only fair to say that Major Weir's reputation as a warlock grew considerably after his death.

Sir George Maxwell and the Witches of Pollokshaws

The story of the sufferings of Sir George Maxwell of Pollok has certain elements in common with the account of the alleged bewitching of Christian Shaw of Bargarran. Like the story of Christian Shaw, it involves events which took place over a period of several months, and concerns an alleged conspiracy of witchcraft against one particular victim. It also involves a young person at a vulnerable age in life. In the case of Christian Shaw, it was she who featured as both accuser and victim. In the case of Sir George Maxwell, the young person was the accuser while he was the victim.

In the winter of 1676, Sir George began to suffer severe pains in his side and in his shoulder, which were accompanied by feelings of intense heat. The onset of the trouble had been quite sudden. He had been staying in Glasgow in October when he had woken up, quite suddenly, in terrible pain. Doctors were at a loss as to the cause or cure of his complaint and the good man had no alternative but to suffer for several weeks as a result of it.

There was a newcomer in the area at around this time – a young girl who, for reasons unknown, had lost the power of speech. Her name was Janet Douglas and nobody knew where she had come from, but after she had been living in Pollok for a few weeks, she got to know Sir George's two daughters and learned of their father's mysterious illness. The girl must have been very adept at using sign language, for she was able communicate to Sir George's daughters that she knew what was causing his trouble. Some time before, a local boy had been caught stealing fruit from Sir George's orchard. The boy claimed that he had had an accomplice, by the name of Hugh Stewart, who had escaped. Hugh Stewart's mother, claimed Janet Douglas, had constructed a figure of Sir George out of wax, and had been sticking pins in it. Her story could be proved, because the waxen image still existed – they would find it in the woman's cottage, concealed at the back of the fireplace.

Sir George's two daughters were sceptical at first, but two of their father's servants offered to help and agreed to accompany Janet Douglas to the house of the woman in question, Janet Mathie. There, the girl was able quickly to find the waxen image which she said would be there. It had two pins stuck in it, corresponding to the areas of pain which had been troubling Sir George. The figure was taken back to Sir George's house and Janet Mathie was apprehended for questioning.

Janet Mathie at first denied the charge against her and tried to place the blame for the construction of the wax figure on Janet Douglas. However, a witch-pricker was summoned, and when Janet Mathie was examined, several 'witch marks' were found on her person.

The wax figure appeared indeed to have been connected to Sir George's illness, for after its discovery, his pains disappeared as quickly as they had come. But in the early days of the following year, while Janet Mathie was still in prison and, presumably, out of harm's way, Sir George fell ill once again, this time so severely stricken with pain that his family feared for his life. Shortly afterwards, a message reached them from Janet Douglas saying that Janet Mathie's eldest son, John Stewart, had made another figure of Sir George, this time fashioned from clay, and had hidden it in his house, under his mattress.

At once a group of men went to the house and searched beneath the mattress on John Stewart's bed. They found a clay figure there, stuck with pins, just as Janet Douglas said that they would. John Stewart stoutly denied that he had made the image, but was taken into custody in spite of his protestations. His younger sister, Annabel Stewart, who was only fourteen years old, was also taken prisoner.

It was Annabel Stewart who finally gave way under questioning. She confessed that she had been in the house when the clay figure was made. Her brother had been there, along with three women: Bessie Weir, Marjory Craig and Margaret Jackson. The Devil himself had also been in the house, in the form of a 'black gentleman'. There were now six people allegedly involved in the conspiracy against Sir George. Annabel was also able to talk about the making of the first, waxen, figure. Her brother John had not been present on that occasion, but her mother and the three other women had been there, along with the Devil, and they had turned the figure of Sir George on a spit over the fire.

John Stewart was examined for witch-marks, which were found. Following this, his attitude changed and he confessed, his story going along similar lines to that of his sister. The description he gave of the Devil was of 'a man dressed in black, with a blue band and white hand-cuffs, with hoggars over his bare feet, which were cloven.'

When Margaret Jackson, Bessie Weir and Marjory Craig were taken into custody and questioned, Margaret Jackson, a frail old woman of eighty, confessed, but the other two still maintained their innocence. When Margaret Jackson was examined for witch-marks, several were found on her body.

While all this was going on, Janet Mathie, the first to be ac-cused, still denying the charges against her, was being held in prison in Paisley. In the middle of January, Janet Douglas informed the authorities that the witches' malevolence was not aimed at Sir George Maxwell alone. His entire family was under threat. She told them another figure had been made by Janet Mathie, not, this time, of Sir George, but of his wife. Janet Mathie's cell was searched and a clay figure of a woman was found underneath the mattress on her bed.

An application was made to the Privy Council for a commis-sion, and the case went to court in January 1677. The three confessants, Annabel Stewart, John Stewart and Margaret Jackson gave detailed accounts to the Commissioners of the Justiciary in Paisley of the events surrounding Sir George Maxwell's illness.

Annabel Stewart had made her pact with the Devil at harvest time the previous year, at her mother's house, and with her mother's and Bessie Weir's encouragement. The Devil had lain with her in her bed and he had felt cold. Several meetings had taken place with the Devil, and he had given each of the women spirit-names. Janet Mathie was Landlady, Bessie Weir was Sopha, Margaret Jackson was Locas and Marjory Craig was Rigerum. All the women had been present when the wax figure of Sir George had been made and roasted over the fire. The Devil himself had placed the pins in the wax figure. The second figure, the clay one, had been made in the January of the following year at her brother's house, where Annabel had been summoned by Bessie Weir. Then, also, the Devil had been present.

John Stewart's confession told of his making the Satanic pact in January, at his own house, on the night on which the clay figure was made. He had been warned by Bessie Weir that the meeting would take place, and the night after she had spoken to him, he had been woken from sleep by a black man. Bessie Weir, Marjory Craig and Janet Mathie had entered the house. Annabel Stewart had arrived at the house later. John Stewart had been urged to renounce his baptism in the accepted fashion, with one hand on the crown of his head and the other on the sole of his foot. He was given the spirit-name of Jonas. The Devil, going by the name of Ejool, had asked for the agreement of everyone present for the clay figure to be made, to take revenge upon Sir George Maxwell for having Janet Mathie apprehended.

Margaret Jackson's account of the making of the two effigies was very similar to that of Annabel Stewart's. She had renounced her baptism and given herself over to the Devil some forty years ago. Like Annabel Stewart, she had lain in bed with the Devil. She had woken during the night before the making of the clay effigy and had been startled to find a man in bed with her. At first she thought it was the figure of her husband, who was long dead, but when the man disappeared she realised it had been the Devil.

Other witnesses gave accounts of the discovery of the two effigies, and of the two bouts of illness which Sir George Maxwell had suffered.

The case against the accused seemed to be very strong. Annabel and John Stewart urged their mother in the strongest terms to confess, but she still refused to admit her guilt. Bessie Weir and Marjory Craig also refused to give in to pressure to confess.

Annabel Stewart was only thirteen and in view of her young age, the court showed her leniency. Her life was spared, but she was imprisoned for her part in the affair – for how long, we do not know.

The five remaining accused were tried and sentenced to death in February, 1677. On the 20th February, they were hanged and burnt at Paisley.

Janet Douglas, the accuser, miraculously recovered the power of speech shortly afterwards. Although few people had any doubt at the time that the five who were executed were guilty, there were concerns about where the young girl had come from, how she had come about her knowledge of the witches' activities and why she had come to Pollok in the first place. She would only admit to having had visions of the Devil and the witches. Some believed this to be evidence that she had been in communication with spirits (which would make her suspect herself), but she denied this. Her 'witch-finding' activities were not confined to Pollok, for she was later instrumental in the apprehension and execution of five accused witches at Dumbarton and was involved in another witch investigation in Stirling. She suffered for her talent in the end, for some time later she was taken before the council in Edinburgh and was scourged and banished.

It might be argued that Janet Douglas was obviously disturbed and her inability to speak and subsequent recovery were purely psychosomatic. She was a young girl, by all accounts alone in the world, and had found herself a friendly association with the Maxwell family. Might her 'witch-finding' have been some sort of bizarre attention-seeking behaviour? She might herself have been responsible for the placing of the images in the places in which they were discovered.

But three of the accused offered to confess, and their confessions were convincingly similar – the spirit-names which the accused had been given, the appearance of the Devil when he was present at the meeting at John Stewart's house, the names of those who had been present. The reliability of these confessions, of course, cannot be judged, for there is no transcript of the interrogations of the accused. There is no way of telling how much pressure had been put on the confessants, or how much, if any of their stories had been suggested to them. One of the confessants was a very elderly woman, another a child of only thirteen. We have no knowledge of their state of mind, but it must be recognised that both might be vulnerable to suggestion on account of their age. All three confessants might have felt – or have been persuaded – that a confession might result in leniency – as it did, in the case of Annabel Stewart.

The truth of the matter will never be known. It was said, that as Bessie Weir, the last to be executed, was taken down from the gallows, a raven flew at the hangman – a sure sign that devilry had been at work. But we have to wonder, as the terrible bonfires burned in Paisley on the 20th February 1677, how many of those watching felt that justice was being done.

The Witches of Bo'ness

In 1679, when witch-fever was showing signs of dying down in other parts of Scotland, one of the last multiple trials to take place for witchcraft sent six people from the area of Bo'ness (then known by its full name of Borrowstoneness) to their deaths. At a time when charges of witchcraft were becoming gradually less frequent and were being treated with greater scepticism than they might have been before, this case was all the more horrifying for the fact that those who were charged and executed had comparatively little charged against them in the way of malefice. The charges against them mostly concerned what appears to have been little more than drunken and libidinous behaviour. Of course, it was established that a Demonic Pact had been made. In addition, it was said that the women had indulged in intercourse with the Devil and that on several occasions, over a period of several years, the accused, five women and one man, had drunk large quantities of ale in the Devil's company.

The accused were Annabel Thompson, Margaret Pringle, Bessie Vicker, William Craw and two women with the same name, Margaret Hamilton. The precise nature of the alleged crimes of William Craw are not clear from documentary evidence of the trial, but it was stated that all of the accused had formally renounced their baptism and entered into a pact with the Devil. The group were then said to have had meetings with the Devil on several occasions after this. Annabel Thompson had first met the Devil just after she had been widowed for the first time, on the road between Linlithgow and Bo'ness. It was on the occasion of her second meeting with him, this time at the Coal Hill, that she had succumbed to his promises of a better life and had given herself over to him, soul and body, in the accepted manner.

The women and William Craw had all met several times in Bessie Vicker's house and had drunk large amounts of ale which had been supplied by Craw and the Devil. Like Annabel Thompson, Margaret Pringle and Margaret Hamilton had also had sexual intercourse with the Devil; in Margaret Hamilton's case, he had been in the form of a black dog. The Devil had left his mark on the woman. He had pinched Margaret Pringle on the arm, and the area where he had pinched her caused her pain for eight days. The discomfort was only relieved when the Devil had touched the spot again, making the pain disappear.

The charges against the group make disturbing reading. Perhaps the accused did believe they were taking part in demonic activities. But it is also quite reasonable to suspect the women were victims of a cruel confidence trick and that William Craw (who generously supplied the ale) played the part of officer whilst an accomplice played the Devil in order to take advantage of lonely, vulnerable widows. Perhaps the accused were no more than a group of sad individuals taking what comfort they could in each other's company; finding some sort of solace in alcohol, partying and sex.

There was only one brief mention of intended harm in the charges laid against the group. At a meeting on Hallowe'en, 1679, the five women and Craw were said to have gathered at Murestane Cross where they danced to music provided by the Devil playing on his pipes. At this particular meeting the group had plotted to destroy a man called Andrew Mitchell of Kinneil – how, or why, we do not know. It is not clear whether they were believed to have succeeded in this, for further details of this alleged malefice were not given, nor was there any mention of actual harm being done to the aforementioned Andrew Mitchell.

Whatever this unfortunate group were guilty of, it is unlikely that their crimes, if any had been committed, were of such severity as to warrant anything like the treatment which they received after the jury – which numbered some forty-five people – had found against them. On the 23rd December 1679, between the hours of two and four (quite a common time for witch executions), all six were led to the Corbiehill to the west of Bo'ness, where they were strangled at the stake and burnt to ashes.

Christian Shaw of Bargarran and the Paisley Witches

Christian was the daughter of John Shaw, Laird of Bargarran. She was eleven years old when the events leading up to one of the most dreadful episodes in the history of Scotland's witch-hunts took place.

In the last week of August 1696, Christian began to display signs of a very disturbing affliction. She began to suffer from violent fits, periods of unconsciousness, pain and contortions of the body. Inbetween these fits, she seemed quite well, but she would be seized with them suddenly, without any warning. Sometimes she appeared to have been rendered completely speechless.

It seemed as if she was fighting off some invisible enemy, and it took considerable force to hold her down, so violent were her strugglings. Doctors were summoned and tried various treatments to no avail. Both during her fits and in periods of lucidity, Christian named Katherine Campbell, who was a maid in the house, and Agnes Naismith, an old widow in the neighbourhood, as being the primary causes of her distress.

It transpired that about a week before the onset of her troubles, Christian had crossed Katherine Campbell. She had caught the maid stealing milk, and told her mother. Katherine Campbell's reaction had been to curse the child: 'The Devil harle your soul through hell.' A few days later, Agnes Naismith, an elderly woman who lived in the district, who was known to be malicious and spiteful and was already suspected of having caused harm through witchcraft, had appeared at the Laird of Bargarran's house and spoken to Christian, enquiring after her health. Within less than two days, Christian had become unwell.

If her behaviour was not borne out of malice, or spite against the two women, and if she genuinely believed herself to be ill, it is quite reasonable to guess that Christian's sickness was of a hysterical nature. She was clearly afraid of these two women and it is possible that she had let her fears get out of hand. But these events took place at a time when it was still widely believed that great harm could be caused to people through a powerful curse, or an evil stare. Christian's hysterical behaviour would thus be reinforced by the credulous reactions of those around her. Christian was taken to Glasgow twice to be examined by eminent physicians, but her symptoms only grew worse. She began to spit hair, feathers, sticks and bones from her mouth. Periods of extreme pain were followed by periods of unconsciousness from which she was apparently unable to be wakened.

In the months that followed, Christian's bizarre affliction

aroused the concern and curiosity of a growing number of people. Agnes Naismith was twice brought to see Christian and on her second visit, prayed for the child. Christian claimed that after that time, Agnes stopped troubling her. Katherine Campbell was asked to do the same, but refused. Christian continued to complain of the torment she was suffering from Katherine Campbell until Katherine was arrested and taken into custody.

But Katherine Campbell and Agnes Naismith were not the only causes of Christian's torment. Over the months of her illness, Christian accused a growing number of individuals of causing her harm. These people, said Christian, were agents of the Devil. They injured her in a variety of ways. Although they were not physically present, she could feel them choking her, hitting, pinching and scratching her. They talked to her and tormented her, threatening her with death should she reveal their names. In the presence of concerned family, ministers and others, Christian would sometimes converse with these people. They wanted her to become a witch, but she was resisting. She was even heard talking to the Devil himself, struggling to resist his evil temptations.

Christian named a number of people. A farmer on her father's land, John Lindsay of Barloch, visited the house one day and his presence seemed to cause Christian great distress. She named him as one of her tormentors. Another caller at the house, a highlander asking for shelter, provoked a similar reaction in the child. Christian's father made both these men touch his daughter and her reactions to their touch was so violent that the laird imprisoned both men at once in his own home.

In January 1697, a Commission was appointed by the Privy Council to carry out an official investigation into the case. Before the first meeting of the Commission, several arrests were made. Alexander Anderson, who had been named by Christian, was taken into custody along with Elizabeth, his daughter. When Elizabeth was questioned she eventually broke down and confessed. She admitted that her father, the highlander and others were guilty of consorting with the Devil, practising witchcraft, and causing harm to Christian Shaw, but she denied her own involvement in any malefice against the girl. Six people were named by Elizabeth; the Highlander, her father Alexander, brothers John and James Lindsay (nicknamed the Bishop and the Curate respectively), Agnes Naismith and Margaret Fulton. These people, once they had been taken into custody, were brought to the Barragan house along with Katherine Campbell and asked to touch Christian in front of the members of the Commission. Each time, at the slightest touch, Christian fell into a violent fit. Along with Agnes Naismith, John and James Lindsay were both already reputed to be warlocks. Alexander Anderson was little more than a beggar, but his daughter was adamant that he had willingly gone into the service of the Devil.

Under further questioning by the Commission, Elizabeth gave further details regarding her involvement in witchcraft. Her grandmother Jean Fulton, with whom she lived, had been a witch. After her grandmother's death, she had taken to the road with her father, who begged for a living. In the company of her father, Elizabeth had met the Devil and had witnessed a frenzied gathering involving those who were now in custody and certain others, namely her two young cousins, Thomas and James Lindsay, John Reid, sisters Janet and Margaret Roger and one other unknown. Elizabeth had been reluctant to participate in the night's activities and had been no more than an onlooker. Other meetings had taken place after that, meetings at which harm was planned and done to various individuals in the neighbourhood. There had been a meeting in the orchard of Bargarran. Plans had been made to kill Christian Shaw. Throughout the whole, Elizabeth maintained stoutly that in spite of her father's encouragement, and to his great annoyance, she had refused to make a pact with the Devil.

More people were taken into custody and questioned, including Elizabeth Anderson's sister Jean, Margaret Lang and her daughter Martha Semple, and the two young Lindsay boys, both vagrants. The elder of the two boys took some finding, for he had left the district. Eventually he was tracked down in Glasgow, confined in the tolbooth on a charge of theft.

Margaret Lang and her daughter were brought before Christian Shaw, as was Margaret Roger, and she confirmed that all three were part of the demonic conspiracy against her. The Lindsay boys, when questioned, confessed that they had seen much of what Elizabeth Anderson had witnessed at the witches' meetings. They named some people that Elizabeth Anderson had named, and some that she had not. Several of these names coincided with those accused by Christian Shaw.

In the end, twenty-four people were named in the application to the Privy Council for a Commission for trial. By the time the trial took place, there were twenty-seven accused. Some of them would eventually be set at liberty. There were now more charges to face than those concerning Christian Shaw. The young Lindsay boys and Elizabeth had spoken of murder having been committed; two young babies in the district had been killed by the witches; one strangled in bed while his parents slept, the other falling mysteriously ill and dying as a result of spells that had been cast. A ferry boat had been sunk, drowning two men, and a minister had also been killed, dying from a fever of unknown origin after the witches had burnt his image over a fire.

The affair dragged on. Christian's behaviour varied from that of a normal, calm child, to that of a demon. During numerous religious services at which she was present, either in her own home or in church, she was liable to be particularly disruptive, laughing and shrieking to drown out the words of the ministers. She could be extremely violent and abusive. At other times, she appeared to take off and fly, as if pulled by an invisible rope. Strange injuries would appear on her body, caused, she said, by the Devil and the witches who wished her harm. And sometimes she seemed to sink into a sort of hypnotic trance, quite peaceful, but oblivious of her immediate surroundings. Perhaps the most disturbing behaviour she displayed was when she appeared to be conversing with the Devil himself. Strangely, though, when those whom she accused were taken into custody, her symptoms eased considerably.

In March, 1697, seven months after the onset of Christian's terrible illness, the trial began.

With so much evidence to be heard and time for adjournments, it took until May for the trial to reach its conclusion. The weight of the responsibility which they bore must have been felt terribly by the Judge, lawyers, ministers and jurors. Between March and May, two more confessions were forthcoming, from Margaret Roger and her sister Janet. Their confessions added to the weight of evidence presented by the prosecution and their professed repentance was to earn them their freedom. Elizabeth Anderson would be released after having given her testimony in court. In spite of the objections of some members of the clergy, the two young Lindsay boys, one barely eleven and the other not much older, were considered too young to be tried in court (although members of the clergy were not in agreement with this) and were also eventually set at liberty. A few others were released on bail and some were detained in prison awaiting further investigation and trial at a later date. Alexander Anderson, Elizabeth Anderson's father, had already died in jail. Seven people were eventually tried. They were Katherine Campbell, Agnes Naismith, the adult Lindsay brothers John and James, John Lindsay in Barloch,

Margaret Lang and Margaret Fulton. Evidence was heard from members of the clergy who had attended Christian Shaw during her illness. Margaret and Janet Roger, Elizabeth Anderson, young James and Thomas Lindsay, the parents of the two murdered babies, Christian Shaw and a number of others were also called to testify. None of the seven accused had shown any inclination towards making a confession or repenting. They all denied the crimes of which they were accused. But they were all pronounced guilty and sentenced to be strangled and burnt. The evidence against John Lindsay in Barloch had been particularly weak, but along with the six others, he was condemned.

The horror of the day of their execution can only be imagined. The sight of the condemned as they went to their deaths, the smell of the burning bodies, must have lingered in the memories of those who were among the watching crowd for a long time afterwards. In total, nine of the accused died. Along with the seven who were executed, and Alexander Anderson who died in prison before he could be tried, John Reid, one of those awaiting trial at a later date, died in mysterious circumstances not long after the executions. There is no record of the others, who remained in prison, ever having faced a trial. They lingered in captivity for at least two years afterwards. Christian Shaw recovered quickly, and completely. Her adult life was a successful one, albeit marred by the death of her husband barely two years after their marriage. Christian took up thread spinning and bleaching and eventually became the founder of the Bargarran sewing thread company.

The case of Christian Shaw's mysterious illness was to become the subject of much heated debate in later years. Had she been an innocent child victim of demonic possession, or were her symptoms psychosomatic – or clever pretence? Were the people who were executed witches, or helpless victims of a child's imagination, or malice?

It is likely that Christian's symptoms were of a hysterical, or psychosomatic nature. But it is also quite possible that she felt that she had something to fear from the people whom she accused – she may have seen, or heard, more than she ought. There had been deaths associated with the case, certainly; two babies and four adults. Whether those who were executed were directly responsible for any or all of these deaths will never be known, but as far as the prosecution lawyers, judge and jury were concerned, the confessions of the Lindsay boys, the Rogers sisters and Elizabeth Anderson were all the proof that they needed. The adult John and James Lindsay had a bad reputation already. What they had done to earn this reputation is not clear, but whether or not they deserved it, it would go a long way towards convincing the jury that they must be guilty in this affair. Katherine Campbell was known to have a wicked temper and a sharp tongue. As in the cases of many other witches tried in different parts of the Scotland, this sharp tongue had been the primary cause of her undoing. Margaret Fulton was a poor old soul, who had completely lost her reason by the time she was executed. Her fate was sealed by the evidence of Margaret and Janet Roger, who had confessed to save their own skins. John Lindsay in Barloch had the least evidence against him. His guilty verdict was based on one fact alone, that Christian Shaw had fallen into a fit when he had touched her. Agnes Naismith, a bitter old woman, with a bad reputation, had nothing to fight against her conviction. And Margaret Lang, whose arrest came as a great surprise to many people who had always regarded her as a God-fearing soul, was now delated as a servant of the Devil by Christian, Margaret and Janet Roger, James Lindsay and Elizabeth Anderson.

We can only wonder what the true facts were that lay behind this tragic episode. We can only be sure of one thing. If Christian Shaw had lived in the twenty-first century and not the seventeenth, her illness would no doubt have been viewed in an altogether different light and those whom she accused of causing her so much pain, whatever else they may or may not have done, would not have found themselves facing death for harming her.

The Witches of Pittenweem

By the turn of the eighteenth century, prosecutions for witchcraft were becoming increasingly rare. But in the East Neuk of Fife, in the fishing village of Pittenweem, it appears that witchfever had not yet burned out.

In 1704, a young boy called Patrick Morton, an apprentice blacksmith who lived in Pittenweem, fell foul of the ill-temper of a woman called Beatrix Laing. She had asked him to make some nails for her, but he had been unable to oblige immediately, his time being taken up with another job on which he was already working. Beatrix took umbrage at his refusal and went away, muttering under her breath. At this point, it seems that the lad's imagination began to take over. He feared that Beatrix was cursing him. Shortly afterwards, when he saw Beatrix tipping hot embers into a bucket of water, he became convinced that she was uttering charms to herself, and assumed that the charms were against him. Some days later, the lad fell ill. He was struck by some mysterious weakness, followed by paralysis and fitting. His body became alarmingly swollen, his head turned to an awkward angle, and he had difficulty breathing. Whatever illness it might have been that Patrick Morton was suffering from, he believed it had been caused by Beatrix Laing. She had bewitched him. He confided his fears to the local minister, Patrick Cowper, and along with Beatrix Laing, he accused another woman called Janet Cornfoot.

Beatrix Laing was the wife of a respectable burgess of the town. Her husband had served as treasurer of the council. But her position in society was not enough to offer her any protection against Patrick Morton's accusations. It is quite possible that she had already been suspected of witchcraft. She was taken into custody for the process of interrogation to begin. The minister Patrick Cowper, eager to have his conviction, proved to be a cruel tormentor and Beatrix was denied sleep for five days, and subjected to torture. At length, the poor woman gave her interrogators the confession they wanted, naming, as she did so, certain other people, including Janet Cornfoot, Isobel Brown and Nicol Adam. Once her torment had come to an end, however, Beatrix withdrew her confession, on the grounds that it had been obtained under unreasonable duress. This did her no good, for she was subjected to further abuse and then thrown into a dungeon, where she stayed for a period of five months while Cowper made application to have her, and others among her co-accused, tried in Edinburgh. Her case never came to trial in the High Court. It seems that, in Edinburgh, reason prevailed and the Privy Council decided against taking the matter any further. Beatrix was ordered to pay a fine and was released. But justice (or justice as he saw it) was still uppermost in the mind of the minister and good citizens of Pittenweem, and upon Beatrix Laing's release, with the blessings of Mr Cowper, an angry mob hounded her out of her home town.

Isobel Adam was also forced to confess, but she too, in spite of her confession, was able to secure her freedom after payment of a fine. Her fate thereafter is not known, but it is reasonable to assume, in the light of Beatrix Laing's treatment, that she, too, found herself banished from the community.

Another of those who had been apprehended, one of the people whom Isobel Adam named in her confession, was a man called Thomas Brown. He died while in prison in Pittenweem – in all probability his death occurred as a direct result of his treatment while in custody.

Of all those who were accused, Janet Cornfoot suffered the most terribly. She was apprehended following Patrick Morton's accusations, tortured and detained for trial. When, along with that of Beatrix Laing, her case was referred to Edinburgh, she was also released, but she was immediately taken into custody in Pittenweem again. Patrick Cowper was determined that she be re-tried and found guilty. The minister must have had a sadistic streak, for he took it upon himself personally to administer the harshest of floggings, in order to force a confession from her. For a short time, it seemed as if Janet might yet be able to save her own life, for somehow, she managed to escape from prison. But as soon as the news of her escape spread through the town, a frantic search was begun, and before long, the terrified creature was found, dragged out from hiding and hauled down to the beach by a raging mob of townsfolk, baying for her blood. All thoughts of true justice had deserted the people of Pittenweem and Janet's neighbours had become her lynch-mob.

Janet's hands and feet were tied, then she was strung onto a rope stretching between a ship in the harbour and the crowd on the shore. Swinging her outstretched body from side to side, the mob hurled stones at her. When the novelty of this had worn off, they untied her and dumped her, battered and bruised, on the shore. Then they placed a heavy door on top of her, piling boulder upon boulder onto the door until all signs of life in Janet's crushed body were finally extinguished. The good minister and the lawmen did nothing to prevent the horror.

The case of the Pittenweem witches is a particularly horrific episode in the history of the Scottish witch-hunts. The records are full of accounts of ill-treatment, cruelty and injustice, but this stands alone as an example of the terrible consequences of mob hysteria. It is all the worse for the fact that the events took place at a time when in most other parts of Scotland, reason was beginning to prevail. In only thirty years' time, the crimes of which Janet Cornfoot and Beatrix Laing had been accused would no longer be recognised in law.

the stuff of Legends

Throughout Scotland's bloody history, frequent religious and political disputes and struggles for power and prestige, both personal and collective, have meant that certain figures have arisen periodically whose names, even after their death, have struck fear into the hearts of many. The reputations of some of these people were such that legends grew up surrounding their lives, which were retold and elaborated upon after their deaths. These were people who possessed a considerable amount of power, which was not necessarily used for the good, and it is understandable that sometimes this power was perceived as being of a diabolical nature. Thus, certain important figures in the story of Scotland came to be associated, in legend, with the Devil and the Black Arts.

Michael Scott – 'The Wondrous Wizard'

Michael Scott was a man of some considerable intelligence and learning. He was born around 1175 and although his birthplace is unconfirmed, he is believed to have come from a Border family. He spent most of his life studying in England and on the Continent and acquired a considerable reputation throughout Europe as a philosopher, astrologer, linguist and translator. He was also known to be interested in magic and in the occult, and it is as a wizard that his name has passed down in legend over the centuries, particularly in the poetry and stories of the Border country. One particular story about Michael Scott concerns his dealings with the Devil, and how, using intelligence and ingenuity,

Scott was able to outwit him. The Devil had sent some of his imps to Michael Scott and had challenged him to find them tasks to do. They would do anything that was asked of them, but they had to be kept perpetually occupied, or the mischief that they might cause was unthinkable. Scott soon realised that the challenge could become a terrible torment, for whatever the task he set the devilish imps, no matter how difficult, it appeared that hardly was his back turned than the job was done and he was forced to think of something else to occupy them. For some days he was troubled by them, setting them task after task, only to find that they were able to accomplish almost anything speedily and without any apparent difficulty. Finally, Scott found a job that would keep the fiendish workers at their labours for all time. He asked them to go down to the shores of the sea and make him twined ropes of sand. The imps rushed off to begin their work, but before the day was out, they found that the task was impossible. They could not mould the fine grains of sand into strong threads, nor could they twist the threads into ropes. And every time they made some progress in their task, the tide would come in and wash their efforts out to sea. But they had to do as they had been asked by the wizard, and so, for evermore, the imps were condemned to spend their time on the shores of the sea, working at a never-ending, impossible task. Scott had played the Devil at his own game, and won.

Michael Scott is believed to have been buried in Melrose Abbey, along with his books of magic, and it is said that the site of his grave is haunted by a ghostly serpent-like creature, crawling along the stone flags of the ruined abbey.

Lord Soulis

William, Lord Soulis, was a powerful Scottish noble, living in fourteenth century Scotland. His family owned considerable amounts of land in the Border country, and he had a claim to the throne of Scotland through his grandfather, Nicholas de Soulis, great-grandson of Alexander II. William Soulis was involved in a conspiracy against Robert the Bruce in 1320 and ultimately had his lands forfeited and was imprisoned in Dumbarton Castle, where he died. But treason cannot have been his only misdemeanour, however, for his reputation in the area from which he came was such that his life and death came to be re-told in local legends that were much more colourful than any historical account. The legend of the death of Lord Soulis has been told and retold many times, but perhaps the most well-known version of the story is the narrative poem, *Lord Soulis*, by Leyden, which was included in Sir Walter Scott's *Minstrelsy of the Scottish Border*.

According to legend, Lord Soulis was more than a terrify-ing figure and a harsh landlord. He was also a sorcerer. Her-mitage Castle, where he lived, was said to be the scene of many horrors. Lord Soulis was said to have superhuman physical strength, to possess the Evil Eye, and to practice his black deeds with the aid of a familiar, which he kept locked in a chest in the vaults of Hermitage Castle. People claimed that he dug up the bodies of unchristened children to use in his spells. His subjects hated him and blamed him for sickness and death in their animals and children, and complained he had treated them with nothing but cruelty and oppression, burning several people who had fallen foul of him out of their homes. They felt they were powerless against him, for their complaints to the king, Robert the Bruce, had so far gone unheeded. Moreover, they feared the consequences of rising against Soulis, for they suspected that he was protected by powerful magic.

The ultimate downfall of Soulis, according to the legend, came about after he kidnapped a young woman named Marion, who was betrothed to the heir of Branxholm. Having surprised her while she was out riding, Soulis forced her into Hermitage Castle and confined her in a dungeon with the intent of coercing her into becoming his wife. The young heir of Branxholm was enraged by the kidnap of his sweetheart, and gathered a group of men to take action against Soulis. His efforts were in vain. His forces were outnumbered by Soulis's men and he himself was captured and taken into Hermitage.

Branxholm was given a terrible choice by his black-hearted captor: either he must persuade Marion to marry Soulis, or he must die, along with his sweetheart. But Branxholm would not relinquish the hope that he might be rescued, and would not relent. Let Soulis hang him from the highest tree in the forest, he said. He would rather die than know he had let his sweet Marion become Soulis's wife. Taking sadistic pleasure in seeing the torment in the eyes of his two young captives, Soulis gave Branxholm time to reconsider.

Meanwhile, Soulis was expecting revenge from Branxholm's supporters. He sent a messenger out to summon additional troops for support. To his dismay, the forces that were gathered were ambushed on the way back to Hermitage, and all save one man were killed. Soulis began to see his chances of success diminishing. He went down to the cellar to the great chest wherein lived his familiar. As was customary when he summoned the creature, he knocked three times on the chest and called for it to come out. The familiar had helped him before; it had told him what to do, and reassured him in times of difficulty. But this time the familiar had no words that were of much comfort to its evil master. It told Soulis that he could not be killed by steel or water, nor could he be hanged with a rope or bound with cords. But Soulis already knew this. And when Soulis asked it to say that he could not be burned with fire, the spirit refused. Instead, it uttered a terrible warning:

'Beware of a coming tree!'

There were no more words of comfort for Soulis. The evil spirit told him he must leave Hermitage and never return. Soulis stormed out of the cellar, throwing the key over his shoulder as he went. He would leave; he knew he had no choice. But he had one last terrible act of revenge to carry out before he left.

He dragged the young Branxholm and Marion from the dungeon where they had been held captive and forced them out of the castle, into the woods beyond its boundaries. Let Branxholm choose the tree from which he could hang. Wherever he chose to die, Marion would be strung up beside him.

The young Branxholm held his courage, for he still had faith that help would come. He let Soulis drag him from tree to tree in the woods, refusing first one, then another, then another as his gallows. All the time, his eyes darted here and there, searching between the trees for a sign that rescue was at hand. Walter would surely come to his aid.

Walter was Branxholm's brother, and Branxholm's faith in him was to be rewarded. Walter had been gathering a band of men together to take revenge on Soulis. The reputation of the black-hearted Lord had already spread far and wide, and had even reached the ears of the king. And when the king had heard of the kidnap of Marion, he was infuriated, for this complaint was the last in a long series of grievances against Soulis that had been brought before him. It was hardly surprising, therefore, that when the supporters of Branxholm sought the advice of his majesty on what action might be taken against Soulis, his patience finally gave way:

'Boil him, if you please, but let me hear no more about him!'

There was no shortage of men to help Walter take action against Soulis, especially after the king had given them *carte blanche* to do with him as they pleased. Knowing that Soulis practised the black arts and had powers to protect himself against attack, Walter also took along with him a wise man, who had a copy of the book of spells of Michael Scott the wizard. With this man's help, they hoped to breach whatever magical defences Soulis was using. Walter and his men approached Hermitage with caution, taking cover in the trees while they planned their next move. Then they heard the approach of Soulis and his captives.

And so it was that when Soulis dragged Branxholm and Marion out into the woods, his attackers were waiting, crouching behind the trees, rowan sprigs in their hands to protect them from the evil they faced.

'Beware the coming tree!'

Branxholm led Soulis right into the trap that was waiting for him. There was a brief but terrible struggle as Walter's soldiers fell upon Soulis and tried to kill him with their swords. Man after man fell dead or wounded as Soulis repulsed the attack, laughing defiantly, his body unscathed in spite of the hundreds of blows that struck him. Those of his attackers who survived the first onslaught then surrounded him, and bound him with ropes. But every time they secured another rope around Soulis's body, the rope would snap as easily as fine thread. In desperation, Walter's men sought the advice of the wise man. It was obviously very powerful magic that was protecting their prisoner. The wise man consulted the book he had brought with him and at last it all became clear: if steel and water, and ropes were useless against such a man, then there was only one answer. Lord Soulis must be boiled in lead.

Lord Soulis met his death on Nine Stane Rig, a small hill close to the castle. A circle of nine standing stones stood guard as his executioners set a massive cauldron on the flames and brought Soulis forward, encased in sheets of lead that had been torn from the castle roof. They forced him into the enormous cooking vessel, then they stood back, watched and waited as the lead around their fearsome captive first melted, then gradually bubbled and boiled. Soulis was dead at last. The people were free of a tyrant and Branxholm had his revenge.

After the death of Soulis, it was said that Hermitage Castle sank several feet into the ground. Its walls were unable to bear the weight of all the wickedness that had lingered within.

Alexander Skene

Alexander Skene lived in Skene house in the north of Scotland in the seventeenth century. Whether or not the things that were said of him were justified in any way, we will never know, but Alexander Skene had a fearsome reputation in the district surrounding his home on the shores of Loch Skene. Locals said terrible things about him: he was a sorcerer, a servant of the Devil, who would dig up and dismember the bodies of unbaptised children from the local graveyard to feed to the four birds which he kept as familiars; a raven, a crow, a magpie and a jackdaw. Fearsome were the black rituals which he performed in the dark cellars of his castle. Alexander Skene had travelled to Italy when he was a young man, it was said, and there, he had studied the Black Arts under the guidance of none other than the Devil himself. When the Devil had tried to take his soul, Skene had tricked him into taking his shadow instead. Now, no matter where he went, by night or by day, no matter how bright the sun, no shadow was cast by his figure. Everywhere he went, his four familiars went too; sinister winged companions on his mysterious journeys. He was a terrifying figure to see, clothed in black, riding across the countryside surrounding his property in a carriage pulled by two black stallions (some say they were headless).

In the darkest hours of the night, when all good men should have been asleep in their beds, it was said that Alexander Skene harnessed his stallions to the carriage and rode out into the blackness for secret assignations with his lord and master, Satan. And every year on Hogmanay, he used his magic for a special journey to see the Devil. He would cast a spell on the waters of the loch, and a thin layer of ice would form over the top. Scarcely thick enough to hold a child's weight, it was all Skene needed to support his carriage and horses as they thundered straight across the loch to their assignation.

Skene's death was even more terrible than his life, according to legend. One New Year's Eve, just before midnight, he called his servant to harness the horses and prepare the carriage for a journey. The servant hurried to do as he was bid, and within a few minutes, was ready to leave. Skene climbed into the carriage and they set off towards the loch, the four birds flying alongside. Approaching the water's edge, Skene uttered some mysterious words under his breath. The waters stilled and froze. The ice stretched ahead like a great grey-blue sheet of steel.

'Drive on at all speed,' Skene ordered his servant, 'but whatever you do, don't look back or we are all doomed.'

The servant cracked the whip and the horses reared up on their hind legs. Then they suddenly took off across the frozen loch, straining every sinew in their bodies as they responded to the urgent commands of their driver and broke into a gallop. They were great, strong beasts, muscular and heavy, but although the ice was thin, their pounding hooves made no impression upon it. On and on across the loch the carriage thundered, a trail of steam rising from the sweating animals. The wide-eyed servant held the reins with trembling hands, half-admiring, half fearful of his master's powers. Before long they were within sight of the far shore; safety was a matter of yards away. Then disaster struck.

Perhaps he had forgotten his master's warning. Perhaps, hearing a sound that startled him, he turned round. The reason does not matter. The servant looked back. As he turned round, he saw the face of Satan sitting behind him, and no sooner had he done so, than the horses let out an unearthly scream of terror and the ice beneath the carriage gave an almighty crack. Seconds later, the carriage turned into a ball of flame and sank beneath the water, taking servant, master and horses along with it. The water hissed and bubbled angrily for a few moments, then all was silent. The last wisps of steam rose into the darkness and disappeared. Skene had gone forever.

Next morning, there was no sign of the tragedy of the night before to be seen in the loch. Not a trace of the coach, its occupants or the horses remained. It was almost as if nothing had happened. But high in the sky above the loch, the more observant passer-by might have noticed one thing, or four things: a raven, a jackdaw, a crow and a magpie.

Robert Grierson of Lag

Robert Grierson of Lag was a terrible enemy of the Covenanters. In his role as a depute sheriff in Galloway, he hunted down the rebels in the hills of the district with dogged persistence, showing little mercy when he had caught his prey. Notoriously, he ordered the summary execution of several individuals whom he had captured, rather than allowing them to face a proper trial. In court, Grierson was equally cruel, and he was among those who sentenced Margaret MacLachlan and Agnes Wilson, the Wigtown Martyrs, to be tied to stakes in the Solway and drowned.

As with other men who possessed a reputation for wielding power with violence, Grierson's spreading notoriety was paralleled by growing rumour, and the word went round that there was something sinister about his power and his activities. Even when he grew old and ill and could no longer cause harm to his enemies, the stories spread, and it was said that during his final illness, when his servants brought him foot baths of cool water to soothe his gout-ridden feet, the unnatural heat of Grierson's lower limbs caused the water to bubble and boil the minute his feet were placed in the basin. After his death, the legend of Grierson grew still more. The following story told about his funeral illustrates the fear that his name invoked.

The funeral of Grierson of Lag, which took place in 1733, was quite a grand occasion. Surviving accounts show that no expense was spared in the provision of food and drink in copious quantities for the mourners. Perhaps the amount of alcohol that was consumed was partly responsible for the story that was told afterwards, we will never know. It was said that from the moment that Grierson's body was placed in its coffin, a raven took up an eerie lykewake of its own, perched on the coffin lid. The raven appeared particularly black and was apparently of evil countenance. All efforts to chase it away were in vain. It stayed with Grierson until the coffin was laid in the grave.

If the raven's menacing presence was not enough to convince the mourners that Grierson had some unholy friends, the events that took place during the funeral procession must have been. The cortege set off, with the raven flying watchfully overhead. Four strong horses pulled the hearse. It was some distance to the churchyard where the burial was to take place, and it is well-known that Grierson, even when old and weak, was a large, heavy man, but these factors were not enough to account for the extraordinary fatigue that the horses rapidly began to display. The hearse had gone no great distance when they began to sweat and strain. In spite of the fact that the poor beasts were working themselves into a lather of perspiration in their efforts to pull the vehicle with its mournful load forward, it was clear that they were finding it harder and harder to make any progress. At length, the horses stopped and could obviously go no further. The followers looked on in consternation. How was the funeral procession to go on? At length, a relative of the deceased, Sir Thomas Kirkpatrick, who had a reputation for black practices, stepped forward and volunteered the services of a set of his own horses. He summoned his stable lad, who brought the beasts out and harnessed them to the waiting hearse. Sir Thomas himself stepped up onto the hearse and took hold of the reins. He urged the horses on with the whip and suddenly they took off as if all the hounds of hell were after them. The others in the funeral procession could only try to keep up as best they could, for the hearse showed no signs of slowing its pace. The hearse careered on towards the churchyard at full speed, the breathless mourners following at a distance. When the mourners finally caught up with the hearse at the churchyard, they stopped in horror at what they saw. The four fine stallions, having reached the churchyard gates, had dropped down dead.

Grierson was safely interred in the cemetery bounds, but long after his death it was said that from time to time, a black coach and horses could be seen, driving at a furious pace across the waters of the Solway. When some sailors who witnessed the fearful sight one stormy night finally found the courage to ask the coachman where he came from and where he was going, the reply struck fear into their hearts:

'From Hell to Dumfries, to meet with Lag!'

John Graham of Claverhouse

Friend to some, foe to many, John Graham of Claverhouse, 1st Viscount Dundee was a soldier of formidable courage. He was known to his supporters as 'Bonnie Dundee', but to his enemies as 'Bluidy Clavers'. It was the reputation that he earned with his enemies that started the legend of his supernatural powers.

Born in 1649, he served for some years as a soldier abroad, in particular in France and Holland. On his return to Scotland, he took up arms against the Covenanters. Despite a humiliating defeat at the hands of the Covenanting forces at the Battle of Drumclog, Graham continued his campaign against them with unabated zeal and less than a month later, routed them at the Battle of Bothwell Brig. In the years that followed he earned a fearsome reputation as one of the leading figures in the persecution of the Covenanters in the south-west of Scotland.

After the arrival of William III in England, Graham turned his attentions to the Jacobite cause. His death in 1689 was considered by his followers to be a heroic and glorious one. After gathering an army of highlanders to meet loyalist troops in battle at Killiecrankie, he led them to victory but was shot and killed himself in the course of the fighting.

Claypotts Castle near Dundee, which Graham had inherited from his father, Sir William Graham of Claverhouse, in 1672, became the centre of rumours even before Graham's death. It was said that when he visited there, Graham had met with the Devil and had taken part in black rituals and demonic orgies. Strange sounds were reported coming from the castle in the hours of darkness, and these were said to be a sign of the devilish deeds that were done within its walls. It was said of Graham that he had made a bargain with the Devil to make himself invincible in battle, and this accounted for his bravery in the face of battle. When Graham was finally killed, it was said that he had not been shot with an ordinary bullet. Instead, knowing of Graham's powers, one of the loyalist soldiers had plucked a silver button from the jacket of his uniform and had used that to bring an end to Bluidy Clavers for once and for all. And for years after his death, every Hallowe'en, Claypotts Castle was said to glow with strange lights, whilst from within, sounds of unholy revelry would filter out to disturb the quiet of the night.

Aleister Crowley

The name of Aleister Crowley stands out from the figures whose legends haunt Scotland's history for a number of reasons. In the first place, although he achieved considerable notoriety in this country, Crowley was not a Scot. He was born in England, in Leamington, Warwickshire. Secondly, Aleister Crowley's sinister reputation was essentially self-generated – he was open, even defiant, in his denial of the principles of Christianity and in his fascination with the occult. Nor was Crowley a figure of a past long gone. He was born in 1875 and was an adult of the twentieth century.

The son of Edward and Emily Crowley, he was baptised Edward Alexander. His parents were Plymouth Brethren, and he was brought up in an atmosphere of the strictest religious piety. His father died when he was eleven, and this event, combined with a revolt against a regime of considerable cruelty at the boarding school which he attended, brought about a change in the young Crowley's attitude. Rejecting Christianity, he turned to the occult and embarked upon a spiritual quest which was to preoccupy him for the rest of his life.

Crowley was extremely intelligent – and intensely proud of the fact – and progressed from school to Cambridge University. He never graduated from there, but his magical career was begun during his years as an undergraduate, when he made the acquaintance of certain others with an interest in the occult. Through his contacts he was introduced to a sect called the Order of the Golden Dawn. Eventually, he fell foul of the sect and of its leader, Samuel Mathers. He branched out on his own, starting an order called the A.A. In later years, he joined the Ordo Templi Orientis, and rose among the ranks to become head of the order. He travelled extensively throughout the world during his life, his passion for extreme living manifest in the multiple affairs he had, the drugs he took in great variety and quantity, his love of and skill in rock-climbing, and above all, his magical studies and practices. He achieved considerable notoriety while still alive, and was expelled from Sicily, where he had founded the Abbey of Thelema, a commune where like-minded individuals could indulge in drug-fuelled sex and magical rituals. He wrote a large number of books over the years, one of the most significant being *The Book of the Law*, the principal message of which he called the Law of Thelema; 'Do What Thou Wilt shall be the whole of The Law'. He claimed to be able to do several things using his magical knowledge and skills, including the invocation of demons and angels, and making himself invisible. Tragedy seemed to dog those who were connected with him; his wife Rose died a raving alcoholic, a child by his mistress and assistant Leah Hirsig (known as The Ape of Thoth) died soon after birth, and a number of people associated with him either became insane, committed suicide or died prematurely. It was the suspicious death of one of Crowley's followers that prompted his expulsion from Sicily.

Supremely arrogant, Crowley revelled in his reputation as 'The Wickedest Man Alive'. He adopted several different names at different times in his life, but took particular pleasure in referring to himself as 'The Beast – 666'. At the height of his perceived magical powers, Crowley claimed he had become a god.

Crowley's connection with Scotland dates from the earlier years of his life in magic – or magick, as he called it, in order to differentiate it from the art of the illusionist. He had been living in a flat in London, but found the situation rather limiting, and had been searching for some considerable time to find a location suitable for the performance of particular magical rituals. These were known collectively as The Operation of the Sacred Magick, the carrying out of which, he believed, would take his skills as a magician to a higher level.

In 1899, Crowley found what he was looking for in Boleskine House, a remote country mansion on the shores of Loch Ness, close to the village of Foyers. He chose the site for its isolation, and for its layout; he needed a room of a suitable size with a northerly aspect to use as an oratory. Boleskine had the added advantage of offering plenty of scope nearby for climbing, cross-country ski-ing, hunting and fishing for those moments when Crowley took time off from his magic.

In his autobiography, *The Confessions of Aleister Crowley*, Crowley made reference to several disturbing occurrences which took place at Boleskine during his performing of the Operation. An unnatural darkness seemed to pervade the oratory whenever he was working in it; mysterious shadows danced around on the terrace outside. His work involved the invocation of several demons, and it appeared that they made their presences felt to more than Crowley himself. One after another, three associates, whom Crowley had asked to join him at Boleskine while his work was in progress, fled from the house in panic. A lodgekeeper nearby, previously a strict teetotaller, had hit the bottle with a vengeance and in an alcoholic frenzy had attacked his wife and children, putting them in danger of their lives.

Crowley resumed his travels after a while, but returned to Boleskine from time to time over the next fifteen years. He noted with glee that his activities caused unease in the surrounding district and that rumours were spreading about him. Sometimes he played practical jokes to fuel the rumours. One of Crowley's jokes was to start a story that a mythical beast was roaming the area and succeeded in convincing some locals that it was worthwhile trying to hunt it. At other times, according to Crowley's *Confessions*, magical forces continued to work their mischief. He claimed that the house became infested with a strange species of beetle, such as could not be identified by scientists. The infestation, he believed, was the work of his enemy from the Order of the Golden Dawn, Mathers. The servants at Boleskine seemed to be continually falling ill. Most of Crowley's hunting dogs fell ill and died without apparent cause. Most frightening of all was when one of the estate workmen attacked Crowley's wife, Rose.

In spite of his efforts at self-aggrandisement, Crowley's following gradually diminished and his money (a large legacy which he had inherited in his twenties had largely funded his excessive lifestyle) ran out. Crowley's life ended in 1947, in abject poverty, in a bedsit in Hastings. He was seventy-two years old, addicted to huge amounts of morphine, and bankrupt.

The legend of Crowley lived on after his death and in the sixties, fascination with 'the Beast' reached a new all-time high when influential figures of rock and pop started to take an interest in his life and works. Crowley's face appears on the cover of the Beatles' *Sergeant Pepper* album. Ozzy Osbourne wrote a song addressed to him. Crowley's writings, and biographies of Crowley, attracted a wide readership. Crowley memorabilia became sought-after merchandise.

Most significantly of all, Jimmy Page, of Led Zeppelin, bought Boleskine House. The rumours surrounding the property, for so long subdued, increased in volume once again. Tales of sex orgies, Satanic rituals and black sabbaths that were said to have taken place there – even although Crowley did not consider himself to be a Satanist, and did not partake in Black Masses – attracted the attentions of the media, and hundreds of heavy metal fans and occultists. The house was said to be connected by an underground tunnel to the graveyard nearby, where bizarre black rituals were rumoured to have been carried out by Crowley and his proselytes. The stories of supernatural occurrences in the district surrounding Boleskine were re-told and embellished, and new ones were invented. Naturally, it was claimed that Crowley's ghost was one of several sinister spectres that haunted the estate. Crowley once more had a crowd of followers.

Nowadays, Boleskine House is a bed and breakfast, whose owners have nothing to do with magic, black or white. But the place still holds a real fascination for 'Crowley-ites', and others with an interest in the occult. Would Crowley's ghost be pleased with the attention? It would undoubtedly be amused, and flattered, but it might well feel misunderstood. Crowley once sued someone for libel, for calling him a practitioner of black magic. Crowley was certainly a practising magician; he was (he claimed) The Beast; it was said he was the worst man in the world. He was bright, egotistical, arrogant, restless, sexually promiscuous, addicted to danger, drugs and notoriety; 'mad, bad and dangerous to know'. But for all the writings he left, for all that can be known about him, it is unlikely that anyone ever was or ever will be able to understand exactly who – or what – the man was. And as for his reputation in Scotland – did he really merit the other title that has been given to him in this country; 'The Other Loch Ness Monster'? The secret lies with the whispering spectres of Boleskine.

witchcraft in poetry and story-telling

Some famous stories of witchcraft and magic have already been told in this book; the story of the milking-peg in the wall, for example, and the legend of Soulis. Tales of magic and devilry of all sorts have provided entertainment at Scottish firesides for centuries, and have provided great inspiration for Scotland's writers, and in particular some of the most respected poets and novelists. Scottish witches, as those who have read *Macbeth* will know, even caught the imagination of the great English bard, Shakespeare. Sorcery and Satan, magic and malefice, these are elements in some of the best-known and loved works of poetry and fiction, and some of the most frequently told Scottish folk tales, old and new.

Poetry

Few Scots children will finish their education without having read *Tam o' Shanter* by Robert Burns, the bawdy narrative poem that tells, tongue-in-cheek, of the dangers of indulging in large quantities of alcohol on Hallowe'en. Tam is a farmer, with a weakness for alcohol and good company, especially on market nights in Ayr when his pockets are full of coins and his friends have gathered in the pub together after a hard day's bargaining. The poem relates the events of one particular market night, when, after having spent many hours drinking with his friends, Tam finally leaves for home.

Tam has been drinking with his friend Souter Johnny, and as the hours have passed and the ale has flowed, he has also become more and friendly with the landlady:

> *'The night drave on wi' sangs and clatter;*
> *And aye the ale was growing better:*
> *The landlady and Tam grew gracious*
> *Wi' secret favours, sweet and precious:'*

At last, close to midnight, Tam decides it is time to leave.

The night is stormy and there is evil in the air, but Tam is well-anaesthetised thanks to John Barleycorn, and has little fear of superstition or rumour. He rides off into the darkness on his grey mare Meg, humming a cheery tune, but keeping an eye out for the bogey men:

> *'Tam skelpit on through dub and mire,*
> *Despising wind, and rain, and fire;*
> *Whiles holding fast his guid blue bonnet,*
> *Whiles crooning o'er some auld Scots sonnet,*
> *Whiles glow'ring round wi' prudent cares,*
> *Lest bogles catch him unawares:'*

On the way home, he reaches Alloway Kirk, an old building situated close to a bridge over the river Doon, which has a well-established reputation for being haunted. As he reaches the kirk, Tam comes across a sight that at once startles and fascinates him; a coven of witches are dancing a riotous reel as the Devil plays his pipes. All around them is the evidence of their evil activities of the night; open coffins, the corpses within holding candles to illuminate the festivities, bodies of unbaptised children, a thief and a murderer. Blood-encrusted weapons – axes, swords, a knife

– have been placed on the altar. Tam cannot help but stop and look, but it is not these gruesome sights which hold his attention the longest. For, as we know, Tam has an eye for a pretty face, and now his eye has fallen upon one particularly attractive young woman, 'ae winsome wench and wawlie', dancing with frenzied abandon, and dressed only in a short shift ('cutty sark'). He is so entranced by the vision before him and gets so caught up in the excitement of the dance that he quite forgets all caution:

> *'Till first ae caper, syne anither,*
> *Tam tint his reason a'thegither,*
> *And roars out: "Weel done, Cutty-sark!"*
> *And in an instant all was dark;'*

At once all hell is let loose and the witches, realising that they have been being watched, turn on poor Tam. He is forced to make a hasty exit. He spurs his horse Maggie on to the bridge, for he knows that witches cannot cross the water, and narrowly escapes the clutches of the screaming horde, poor Maggie losing her tail to the bold 'Cutty Sark' in the process.

Tam o' Shanter is a humorous tale, written at a time when 'witch fever' had long burned out in Scotland. It is based on a witch story that was told around the area of Alloway, where Burns himself lived. The rattling pace at which events unfold in the poem, the comical reference to Tam's wife, sitting at home 'nursing her wrath to keep it warm' as she waits for him to return, and the descriptions of Tam's all-too-human failings (wine, women and song) in Burns' characteristic colourful linguistic style, all contribute to the poem's abiding popularity with adults and children alike.

Tam o' Shanter has a moral, but it is delivered in playful tone.

In stark contrast to this, some of the poetry that has been written on the subject of witches and witchcraft is much darker, bleaker and more cruel.

The Witch of Pittenweem, a traditional ballad by David Vedder tells another kind of tale; of the life and death of an old witch from Fife. This witch has none of the attractions of the witches in *Tam o' Shanter*; she is ugly, goggle-eyed, with wrinkled skin, a big nose and hunched shoulders. She shuns the light of day and hides away far from town at the crossing of two roads. All that might be feared of a witch is true about this old hag. She has renounced her baptism and taken Satan as her lord and master. She carries a staff made from gallows wood and suckles the Devil's imps at her own breast. She is the cause of sickness and death amongst animals and people and has cast fear into the hearts of everyone around. At last, she is brought to justice. She is pricked for the devil's mark, kept from sleep and tortured. She is ducked in the loch nearby. Finally, she is tied to a stake and the fire beneath her is set alight. But the Devil still has work to do, for a sudden rainstorm puts out the fire as soon as it is lit, and it is only when a monk takes a taper lit from the lamp at St Mary's shrine and relights the fire that the evil woman is finally sent to her doom. This ballad is no humorous fable; it is a horror story in verse. The witch conforms to all one's worst ideas of what a witch might look like. Her wretched fate at the hands of her accusers is the worst that a woman of her like might expect.

Some of the poems that have been written on the subject of Scotland's witches have their origins in fact. *The Witch-Wife's Son* is one such poem. It tells the story of Grissel Jaffrey, one of the last witches to be burned in Scotland, believed to be the last to be burned in Dundee. She was the wife of a brewer and respectable burgess of the city, James Butchart. There are no records surviving of the trial of Grissel Jaffray, so the details of the accusations that were made against her are not known, but the Privy Council issued a Commission for her trial in November 1669, stating that if she could be made to confess,

'without any sign of torture or other indirect means used,'

or failing that,

'otherwise that malefices be legally proven against her',

she should be condemned to death. Whether the poor woman was persuaded to confess or was found guilty purely on the evidence of others is not known, but it did not take long for her dreadful fate to be decided. She was declared guilty as charged and was executed less than two weeks later.

It was said that Grissel Jaffery and her husband had a son, who had gone to sea and had become captain of his own vessel. According to local tradition, the young man was away at sea when his mother was brought to trial and knew nothing of her apprehension for witchcraft or her imminent execution until he sailed his ship in towards Dundee on the day on which she was due to be burned. Tragically, he arrived in port just in time to witness her dying moments from his ship.

The *Witch-Wife's Son* takes up the tale as the sailor is steering his ship towards his home town, looking towards land, thinking of his mother who should be waiting on shore to greet him. As the ship draws closer to port, the sailors realise something out of the ordinary is happening. There are hundreds of people gathered together on the shoreline, and the men on the ship wonder why. It is unlikely to be a welcome party, after all. Then someone spots a lick of flame, rising from the midst of the crowd on the sands at the Seagate. As the flames rise, Grissel Jaffrey's son guesses that a witch is being burned. As his ship draws even nearer to shore he catches sight of the face in the flames and realises with grief and horror that he is looking at his mother.

> ' "*Now, rin the ship in fast, my mates,*
> *At land I fain would be;*
> *That surely was my mither's face,*
> *That face in agony.*" '

He is too late to save her and rants helplessly at the people responsible for his mother's death:

> *'A voice cam' frae the gude ship's side*
> *A voice of agony –*
> *"God's bitterest wrath upon ye bide,*
> *Ye fause loons o' Dundee!*
>
> *"God hide, In His great Judgement Day,*
> *His holy face frae ye,*
> *Wha've ta'en, wi' rash and murderous hands*
> *My mither's face frae me!*" '

Broken-hearted and bitter, he orders his ship to turn about and sail away from the city, never to return. He is deprived of his mother, and the families of the sailors on his ship, waiting for their return are deprived of their husbands, fathers, brothers and sons.

There are numerous tales of witches and warlocks from all parts of Scotland, some loosely based on historical incidents, others pure fiction, which have been handed down both orally and in print over the years. Like older versions of the modern urban myth, some of these tales, told in one particular part of Scotland, and said to relate to real incidents which took place in the area, will have 'doublers'; stories almost identical in detail that are told in other parts of the country.

There are a number of very similar tales that are told of witches transforming themselves into beasts, in particular hares and cats, suffering some injury whilst in animal form, and then being discovered when the injury remains after they have changed back into human form. One of these originates in Morayshire, and tells the story of the Earl of Brodie and his encounter with a magical hare.

The Earl of Brodie and the Hare

The Earl of Brodie was a keen huntsman and spent many long hours in the countryside near Brodie Castle hunting for game. One day, as he was hunting deer in the forest, he came across a hare that was unlike any he had ever seen before. Instead of running away at the sight of a human, as any other hare would do, this particular creature seemed to be taunting him, remaining right where it is, in full view of the Earl, daring him to do his worst. The Earl shot at the hare a number of times, but although he was a marksman of considerable skill, he was unable to hit it. The bullets flew past, and the hare stared back at him, apparently unafraid. Perplexed and frustrated at this turn of events, the Earl took a few more shots at the defiant creature. Although he was sure he had managed to hit the hare, it appeared to be uninjured and still did not run away. At last, the Earl realised that this creature was no ordinary hare and that, therefore, no ordinary bullet would be effective against it. He pulled a silver coin, a sixpence, from his pocket, and loaded his gun with it. Taking careful aim, he fired at the animal one last time. This time, at the sound of the gun firing, the hare leapt into the air with a scream and started to run. The Earl, much to his delight, saw that it was limping; he had managed to wound it in the leg with the sixpence. The hare disappeared into the undergrowth, but the Earl followed the trail of blood left by the wounded creature and found that it led to a cottage not far away. The cottage was the home of an old woman who had a long-standing reputation for mischief. Entering the cottage, the Earl found her huddled up in bed, clearly in pain. In spite of her protests, he threw back the bedclothes and saw that the woman had a wound in her leg, from which the edge of a silver coin was protruding. So she was the hare who had tried to spoil his morning's hunting! Demanding his money back, he pulled the coin from the witch's leg and strode out of the cottage in triumph. The witch must have felt fortunate to escape with her life after the incident; she would not torment the good Earl again.

Another well-known tale concerning shape-changing comes from the Highlands of Scotland. It is called The Witch of Laggan.

The Witch of Laggan

A man from Badenoch was out for a day's hunting in the forest of Badenoch. The weather was bad, and a storm was blowing in, so after a successful morning's activity, he stopped to take shelter and rest in a bothy in the forest. As he sat and warmed himself in front of the fire, his peace was suddenly disturbed by his two hunting dogs, growling and snapping at the door. The hunter restrained the dogs and opened the door. A black cat slunk in past his legs, crept into the corner and cowered there, sodden and shivering. To the hunter's surprise, the cat spoke to him, and told him that she was a poor witch, who had fallen foul of the other members of her coven, and needed his help. The hunter was a great enemy of witches, but was moved to take pity on the wretched creature and invited her to warm herself by the fire. 'The dogs will tear me to pieces if I come closer,' said the cat, but I will be safe if you tie them with this long hair.' The hunter, still unsure of his strange visitor, tied the dogs to a beam in the roof with the hair which the cat had given him, but did not make the knot secure.

The cat moved over to the fire and began to warm herself. As the hunter watched the cat, stretched out in front of the flames, he could see that she was beginning to grow. He commented on this jokingly, but the cat replied that it was only the heat of the fire making her hairs expand. The hunter became more and more anxious as the cat continued to grow at an alarming rate. She continued to grow until she was almost as large as the hunter himself, and then all at once, the cat disappeared and in her place stood a woman, whom the hunter recognised as the Goodwife of Laggan.

'Hunter of the Hills,' declared the foul woman, 'your day of reckoning has come.'

The witch told the hunter that she and other members of her evil sisterhood had caused a death already that day; they had drowned another man, Macgilliechallum of Raasay. Macgilliechallum's name was familiar to the hunter; like him, he had been an enemy of witches. Having had her revenge on one enemy, the witch had now come for another.

The witch moved towards the hunter, but as she did so, the dogs broke free and set upon her, sinking their teeth into her chest and her leg. The witch tried to secure the magical hair which should have kept them tied. 'Fasten, hair, fasten!' she cried. The hair fastened itself round the beam again, pulling the dogs back with it. Tighter and tighter became the knot as the hair obeyed the witch's commands, until finally it snapped the beam in two. Once again the dogs set upon the screaming witch, tearing at her flesh. Shrieking with terror and struggling violently, the evil woman finally changed herself into the form of a raven, and flew out of the bothy and off into the distance. The hunter's two beloved dogs collapsed with exhaustion and died at their master's feet.

With trembling hands and a heart full of sorrow, the hunter set about the task of burying his beloved dogs. Then he turned his back on the bothy and the horrors of the day, and set off for home.

When he got back to his house, the hunter found that his wife was not at home. She returned shortly afterwards and told him that she had been visiting the Goodwife of Laggan, who had been taken suddenly and severely ill that day. It was thought that she would not survive. The hunter at once declared that he too should go and visit the sick woman, and set off there and then to the house where she lived. When he got there, he found several other people had gathered, preparing to mourn a neighbour whom they had held in high regard. The Goodwife was in great pain, and it looked as if she would die at any moment. The assembled company were therefore greatly surprised when the hunter strode over to the bedside and angrily dragged back the covers, to reveal the terrible wounds which his dogs had inflicted. He turned his face away from the hideous sight, and spoke to the startled watchers. Pointing to the witch's blood-soaked body as evidence, he declared that the woman whom so many had come to mourn was an evil witch, who had been responsible for the death of Macgilliechallum that very morning and had tried to kill again in the afternoon.

The witch suddenly became penitent. With her last reserves of strength, she admitted that she had been seduced into the company of witches and service of Satan. She gave a full account of everything, from the first moment of her temptation to the terrible events of the day, in the hope that it might be a warning to others. She expressed the utmost sorrow and regret for all that she had done, and when her confession was finally complete, she gave one last terrible moan, and died.

That night, two travellers in the area were startled by the sight of a woman running in the direction of the churchyard of Dalarossie. She was covered in blood, and she was being pursued by two black dogs. No sooner had the woman and the dogs disappeared from sight than a dark stranger appeared, riding a black horse. The stranger asked the travellers whether they had seen the woman or the dogs. When they replied that they had, the stranger then asked them whether they thought the dogs would have caught up with the woman before she reached the churchyard at Dalarossie. Yes, said the travellers, the dogs were running at great speed and would likely have caught up with the woman quite easily. The stranger rode off, in the same direction as the woman.

The travellers continued their journey, but they had not gone much further when they saw the figure of the dark rider once again, travelling in the opposite direction, with a sinister burden on his steed. Across the bow of the saddle lay the corpse of the old woman, with the two dogs fastened by their teeth to her leg and her breast.

The travellers reached their lodgings for the night and described what they had seen. In return, they were told the story of the witch of Laggan. After death, it seemed, the old woman had been trying to seek sanctuary from Satan in Dalarossie kirkyard. But it was now clear that she had not reached safety in time.

Another witch tale that has been told in different parts of Scotland illustrates the belief that witches were able to fly, and could transform plant or animal matter into magical steeds to carry them through the air as they went about their wicked business.

The Lady and the Horse

There were once two brothers, who were working as stable boys in the service of a wealthy Scottish landowner. The landowner's wife by day was a true lady in every respect, but by night she lived another life.

The older of the two lads was getting worried about his younger brother. On more than one occasion, he had woken in the morning to find his brother lying in his bed beside him looking ill; his body was badly bruised and he was clearly exhausted, as if he had been taking part in some sort of strenuous and violent activity during the night. When the older brother's worries finally led him to question the younger, the young lad denied having left his bed at all during the night, but did say that he had been having a recurrent dream. Every time he had the dream, the lad would wake up the next day feeling dreadful. He dreamt that he had changed into a horse, and that he was being ridden through the air at a furious pace, fiercely spurred on by an unseen rider. The dream always took the same course. The lad would be ridden for a great distance until they finally arrived at a place that was unfamiliar to him. He would be tethered in the darkness of a strange stable and left there for some hours, with neither food not drink. Then the mysterious rider would return, untether him, re-mount and spur him on to return at the same breakneck speed. The boy could remember nothing else, except for the fact that when he woke up, he would be covered with bruises and aching with fatigue.

The older brother suspected that something evil was at work, and made up his mind to stay awake while his brother slept. Some nights later, he was lying beside his brother in the darkness when the stable door opened and their mistress, the lady of the house, crept in, a bridle in her hand. It was clear that it was not a horse that she was after, for she left the horses standing in their stalls, and moved instead towards the place where the young lad lay sleeping. Silently, she slipped the bridle over the boy's head, and at once he was changed into a magnificent young stallion. The boy's brother watched in amazement as his mistress led him out of the stable, mounted, and few off into the darkness.

It was almost light when they returned. The lady led the horse, sweating and panting, towards his brother's bed. Then she removed the magical bridle and the horse became the boy once again, falling onto the straw mattress in an exhausted sleep.

The older boy was enraged to see his younger brother treated in this way, and resolved to take revenge on his mistress. He assured his brother that he would put an end to the strange dreams that had been tormenting him. Then he asked to change sleeping places with him.

Some nights later, the older boy was lying half-awake and half-asleep on his brother's mattress, when he heard the sound of the stable door opening once again. Through half-closed eyes, he could just make out the figure of the lady moving towards him, but he lay perfectly still, and pretended to be asleep when she placed the bridle around his head. She led him out of the stable and then jumped onto his back, digging her heels into his sides and urging him on into the air.

The journey was long and the boy-horse was forced on at a furious pace, so that when they finally stopped, he was gasping for breath; his heart was pounding and his body was slippery with sweat. He allowed himself to be tethered in a darkened stable, but as soon as the lady had gone, he started to rub his head against the stable wall, loosening the straps of the bridle around his head. He knew he had time on his side, for his brother had told him that the lady was always away for several hours. At last, he managed to remove the bridle from his head. No sooner had he done so than he returned to human form. Bridle in hand, the lad crouched down behind the stable door and waited for the woman to return.

Two hours or so before the break of dawn, the latch on the stable door clicked. As the door opened and the lady moved into the doorway, the boy pounced, and flung the bridle over her head. Just as he had done, she changed instantly into a horse. Now was the time for revenge. The boy grabbed a whip that was hanging on the stable wall, and leaped onto the horse's back. He rode the horse harder than he had ever ridden a horse in his life before. He jerked the bit cruelly in the horse's mouth, cracked the whip again and again and hammered his heels constantly into her sides as they charged through the night. The boy rode and rode until he could see the first signs of dawn breaking in the sky. Then he returned to his mistress's house, and outside the front door, he removed the bridle. The horse became the lady again and she collapsed, unconscious, on the ground. Without a sound, the boy turned away and slipped back to his bed in the stable.

The two brothers rose as usual for their duties, and carried on with their work as if nothing has happened, but strange stories were circulating among the other servants of the household. Something terrible had happened to her ladyship, they said. She had been found outside the house early in the morning in a state of extreme exhaustion, her mouth bruised and bleeding, signs of a terrible beating about her body. No-one knew how she came to be there, nor who did this to her. The two brothers smiled at each other. Their secret was safe, for their mistress could never admit anything of her nocturnal activities. They also knew that she would never again try to abuse her stable lads in such a manner.

scottish witchcraft in the twenty-first century

Walk into almost any bookshop in Scotland today and you will be able to find a wide variety of books devoted to subjects which once, in sixteenth and seventeenth century Scotland in particular, would have been condemned as witchcraft. The shelves will be packed with works on subjects as diverse as astrology, Feng-shui, voodoo, Tarot, the I-Ching, Wicca, crystal healing, spiritualism, shamanism and Druid magic. All of these involve one or more of the kind of practices that sent so many people to their deaths following the Witchcraft Act of 1563: healing, charming, foretelling the future, talking to spirits, etc. For a few pounds you can find out about shape-shifting, love spells, candle magic or whatever takes your fancy. It is a sobering thought that the great numbers of people who take an active interest in such things nowadays would, three centuries ago, have been risking accusations of working in the service of Satan.

Few of the people who are interested in astrology, Tarot, or the I-Ching are likely to think of themselves as witches. Even those who dabble in matters occult such as consulting a medium or a healer, attending a séance, performing a simple magical ritual, do not necessarily do so believing that what they are doing is witchcraft.

There are many people, on the other hand, who profess themselves to be practising witches. Some of them will claim that their magical knowledge, rituals, charms and spells are the same as those that were used in Scotland in the time of the Picts.

A variety of magic falls under the general umbrella term of Wicca. Several people claim that their magical skills are hereditary. Like those who practise the nature-based, so-called traditional magic, they believe their craft has been passed from generation to generation, but unlike the traditionalists, those who practice hereditary magic claim that their craft has come to them through family connections, either by blood or by marriage. Some Wiccans follow the Gardnerian tradition, a system revived (or invented) by Gerald Gardner in the 1940s, whilst others follow the Alexandrian tradition, named after Alexander Sanders, a famous figure in the sixties. There are still others; those who practise Celtic magic or Fairy magic, those who give no name to their craft and work alone. Some practitioners of witchcraft refer to deities, whilst others celebrate Nature, and/or the Divine within themselves.

Then there is Druidry, which also covers a wide variety of beliefs and practices. Although it is nature-centred, there are pagan branches of Druidry, and other branches to which self-professed Christians belong.

Although some might argue the contrary, there is unlikely to be any form of magic practised in this country that can be proven to be purely, traditionally Scottish.

We have seen to some extent how magical beliefs and practices changed in the past, adapting to circumstance; as religious beliefs changed, so did those about witchcraft, and as foreign ideas and beliefs about witchcraft reached these shores, so witchcraft lore and witchcraft practices altered to integrate them into the whole. Once upon a time, magic was practised without any reference to the Devil. Then came a time when both those who condemned witchcraft and many of those who practised it believed that Satan was at the root of everything that they did.

In the twentieth century, an open revival in interest in witch-craft made people look back to times when magic was practised outwith the context of a Christian God, and to develop their own form of the craft, based on what they knew of the past. Pre-Christian, pagan magic was seen as the only true craft. But inevitably, no matter how closely anyone might try to follow the principles of ancient magic, their practice would be influenced, firstly by their personal reasons for turning to witchcraft (i.e, what they hoped to achieve) and their own choice, or invention, of rituals to suit their own ends. Moreover, it is hard to distinguish between beliefs and practices that are genuinely ancient and those that are the inventions of a more recent past.

Aleister Crowley, whether he was a black or white magician, practised an eclectic craft. He used the I-Ching, he read Tarot cards, he studied and practised magic from cultures all over the world. This eclecticism is also common in the practice of many Wiccans in Scotland today.

Wicca is generally introspective. It is also a benign, 'white' craft. Whether they practise atheist or pagan witchcraft, its practitioners have nothing in common with those who profess to be Satanists. Whereas in the times of the witch-hunts, all witchcraft was believed to be Satanic, nowadays a distinct line has been drawn between Satanism and Wicca, the former involving Devil-worship, the latter making no reference to the Devil either in belief or practice. Wicca is practised openly and freely (although it has its share of critics, particularly within the Christian church), whilst Satanism is essentially an underground cult, either ridiculed, condemned or feared by the majority of people.

Witchcraft is greatly different from what it was in the sixteenth and seventeenth centuries. Quite possibly, had they lived in more

179

enlightened times, many of those who were drawn to witchcraft in those days might never have resorted to it in the first place. Tongue in cheek, we might argue that many of the witch practices of those days are redundant in modern times. Meteorologists can predict the weather (with reasonable accuracy). Food stealing can be done in any corner shop or supermarket for those who consider such behaviour acceptable, and milk can be lifted off the neighbour's doorstep. Doctors and surgeons are the ones to whom most people turn when illness or injury lays us low, and there are also several widely accepted forms of alternative therapy to support orthodox medical treatment; homeopathy, acupuncture, reflexology and aromatherapy to name but a few. Even love can be viewed in logical terms: hormones, pheromones, the science of sexual attraction. Can't find a partner? Turn to a dating agency to consult a computer database of hopefuls. And as science has developed and enlightenment has dawned, we no longer need to fear the angry look, or the curse. If we want to find out why someone has fallen ill, or why a farmer's crop has failed, we turn to the empirical knowledge and practical resources of the relevant science.

But, in spite of all that science can tell us, in spite of our own knowledge of the practical steps that we might take to preserve our good health and make changes in our lives for the better, there will still be those among us who cling to the belief (or hope) that there are other unseen powers, within us and without, that we can tap into to see into our future and to change it for the better. As long as people think that way, witchcraft will flourish.

index